"To become the best decathlete in the world, you must surround your-self with coaches who think outside the box and who are ready to do things differently. If you don't, chances are, you will end up like your competitors. This book is all about that; it dives into concepts beyond traditional coaching methods. *Team Chemistry* represents very well how my coaches operate: keep an open mind, challenge the status quo and get creative to find a competitive edge."

— DAMIAN WARNER, DECATHLETE, 2020 OLYMPIC GOLD MEDALLIST

"Sport leaders play such an important role to ensure team success. My favourite coaches weren't only great technicians and tacticians; they communicated clearly, instilled confidence and cared about the players. *Team Chemistry* will be a valuable part of a coach's toolkit."

— LAURENT DUVERNAY-TARDIF, NFL GUARD, SUPER BOWL LIV CHAMPION

"Lachance and Ménard show us that building team chemistry one ath-lete, one staff member, one practice, and one day at a time is about more than just the results on the scoreboard. It is a skill that coaches at any level can learn and their book provides the tools to do so. *Team Chemistry* will become a trusted resource for coaches in every sport."

— DANIELLE GOYETTE, THREE-TIME OLYMPIAN, EIGHT-TIME
WORLD CHAMPION, PLAYER AND COACH, HHOF 2017

"I have been fortunate enough to work with and observe many talented coaches, the vast majority of them possessing great content knowledge and ability to teach their craft. However, the highly successful coaches were the ones who also invested their time and bandwidth in building a truly superior culture. *Team Chemistry* provides the tools and tech-niques to help sport leaders foster an elite culture, a culture of respect and responsibility that will in turn help players and staff reach their opti-mal performance. A terrific book that both aspiring and veteran coaches should read and put to use."

— KAI CORREA, COACH, SAN FRANCISCO GIANTS, MLB

"Creating a healthy culture goes hand in hand with developing how you play, your tactics and strategies, and might even be the most important part of a coach's job. Just like the players we work with, coaches can always improve. *Team Chemistry* enhanced my thinking in this space and provided me with new ideas for creating the best environment for my players, my staff, and myself."

— BEV PRIESTMAN, HEAD COACH, TEAM CANADA WOMEN'S SOCCER,
2020 OLYMPIC GOLD MEDALLIST

"For as long as organized team sports have been around, coaches have asked the same questions — how can I encourage a group of individuals to value a set of standards, and how can I create an identity that is unique to our team and our environment? How can we win, not just this game or this year, but sustained success over time? *Team Chemistry* provides important insights and strategies on the complexities of these age-old questions and simple solutions to make your team and culture more robust. A must-read!"

— DEREK JOHNSON, PITCHING COACH, CINCINNATI REDS, MLB

"I can't say enough about this excellent book. Having coached and managed collegiate and professional football players for almost 30 years, I know how important it is to put as much energy into building a positive team culture as I spend on the X's and O's. *Team Chemistry* provides the tools that anyone in a sports leadership role — on the sidelines or in the front office — can use to make their team better."

— DANNY MACIOCIA, VANIER CUP AND GREY CUP
CHAMPIONSHIP-WINNING COACH, GM, MONTREAL ALOUETTES, CFL

"Transitioning from an Olympic figure skater to a coach is a challenging feat. It is important in my new role to educate myself and train my skills, just like I did as an elite athlete. Because *Team Chemistry* is filled with practical tools, it will become a go-to resource for years to come."

— SCOTT MOIR, FIGURE SKATER AND COACH,
THREE-TIME OLYMPIC AND WORLD CHAMPION

"As coaches we dream of our teams playing in perfect harmony. But to get our athletes to reach their potential and for the group to work in unity it takes the common and concerted effort of so many. *Team Chemistry* offers valuable tools to help coaches orient their work and save time and energy by enabling strategies to maximize the rendement of everyone involved in developing a culture of excellence."

— GLENN HOAG, HEAD COACH, TEAM CANADA 2020
OLYMPIC MEN'S VOLLEYBALL

"The life of a coach surprises you every day and the tools in *Team Chemistry* empower the sort of communication, cohesion, and cooperation that can help all sport leaders achieve their goals and realize their potential. Whether selecting staff, finessing a team towards better cooperation, seeking better ways to present ideas, or searching for a different way to approach an underperforming player, this book provides answers. There is wisdom on every page . . . I urge you to read it."

— RIC CHARLESWORTH, OLYMPIC AND WORLD CUP GOLD MEDAL-WINNING
COACH, AUSTRALIAN NATIONAL MEN'S AND WOMEN'S FIELD HOCKEY

TEAM
CHEMISTRY

30 ELEMENTS FOR COACHES TO FOSTER COHESION, STRENGTHEN COMMUNICATION SKILLS AND CREATE A HEALTHY SPORT CULTURE

André Lachance

AWARD-WINNING PROFESSOR AND NATIONAL TEAM COACH

Jean François Ménard

MENTAL PERFORMANCE COACH OF OLYMPIC CHAMPIONS

Editor for the Press: Jennifer Smith
Cover design: David A. Gee

LIBRARY AND ARCHIVES CANADA CATALOGUING
IN PUBLICATION

Title: Team chemistry : 30 elements for coaches to foster cohesion, strengthen communication skills, and create a healthy sport culture / André Lachance, award-winning professor and national team coach ; Jean François Ménard, mental performance coach of Olympic champions.

Names: Lachance, André (Baseball coach), author. | Ménard, Jean François, 1982- author.

Identifiers: Canadiana (print) 20210388854 | Canadiana (ebook) 20210388919

ISBN 978-1-77041-640-6 (softcover)
ISBN 978-1-77305-943-3 (EPUB)
ISBN 978-1-77305-944-0 (PDF)
ISBN 978-1-77305-945-7 (Kindle)

Subjects: LCSH: Coaching (Athletics)

Classification: LCC GV711 .L33 2022 | DDC 796.07/7—dc23

We acknowledge the support of the Canada Council for the Arts. *Nous remercions le Conseil des arts du Canada de son soutien.* This book is funded in part by the Government of Canada. *Ce livre est financé en partie par le gouvernement du Canada.* We acknowledge the support of the Ontario Arts Council (OAC), an agency of the Government of Ontario, which last year funded 1,965 individual artists and 1,152 organizations in 197 communities across Ontario for a total of $51.9 million. We also acknowledge the support of the Government of Ontario through the Ontario Book Publishing Tax Credit, and through Ontario Creates.

PRINTED AND BOUND IN CANADA   PRINTING: MARQUIS   5   4   3   2   1

TABLE OF CONTENTS

SECTION 2: COMMUNICATION

PROVIDING APPROPRIATE FEEDBACK, ADDRESSING WHAT MATTERS MOST AND UNDERSTANDING THE TEAM'S NEEDS

SECTION 3: COLLABORATION

FORMING ROBUST COHESION, CONNECTING AUTHENTICALLY AND SUPPORTING EACH OTHER

SECTION 4: COORDINATION

IMPLEMENTING GROUND RULES, MANAGING CRITICAL SITUATIONS AND DOING THINGS DIFFERENTLY

TEAM CHEMISTRY

1 KM — Kilometre Zero	**5** Welcome	**8** Pygmalion	**11** P.R.P	**14** 5:1	**16** Sociogram	**18** Buddy System	**21** We	**24** Black Box	**27** Hatchet
2 Brand	**6** Oops	**9** Your Coach	**12** Debrief	**15** Lego	**17** Get Personal	**19** Inner Teams	**22** Together	**25** Crisis	**28** Hashtag
3 Team Cycles	**7** Leader(of the)Ship	**10** How Are You?	**13** Win/Lose			**20** Be a Clown	**23** Extra Mile	**26** One-on-One	**29** Goal Getting
4 Staff									**30** M?P
CREATION		**COMMUNICATION**			**COLLABORATION**			**COORDINATION**	

INTRODUCTION

NOVEMBER 13, 2019 —
PALACIO DE LAS CONVENCIONES, HAVANA, CUBA

I had just finished giving my keynote address in a conference room. My presentation highlighted the leadership principles I use as a baseball coach. I collected all of my belongings before leaving the stage to take a seat and listen to the next speaker. Scheduled every two years, this international conference showcases the latest research and best practices in the world of elite sport and physical activity.

The trip to Havana the day before was an interesting journey. Leaving from Ottawa, Canada, I missed my connecting flight and ended up arriving in Cuba very late at night. The lack of sleep made it very difficult to listen attentively to the presentations following mine.

One presenter in particular did not help the cause. Not only did he speak in a monotonous voice, but his presentation was filled with abstract theoretical concepts. It was not very engaging — I had to fight hard to camouflage the yawns that kept creeping up on me.

This presentation brought back painful memories of my high school chemistry classes — atoms and molecules were not my cup of tea. My science mark did not get any better in college. My parents forced me to study hard sciences because back in the day it was well known that studying hard sciences would lead to job opportunities.

Big mistake.

I scored 17 percent on my first chemistry exam. Luckily, the professor was nice enough to let me retake the exam. I ended up doing a little better: 25 percent. This result prompted an expedited visit to the guidance counsellor's office for a change of program. From then on, I had no interest in anything related to chemistry concepts.

Despite disliking the subject, I did retain a few positive memories of playing around with Bunsen burners, test tubes and beakers during chemistry lab sessions. I could relate to the experiments because they were hands-on. As a predominantly visual learner, I was also captivated by something else in chemistry class: the periodic table of elements.

This well-known visual chart, created in 1869 by Russian chemist Dmitri Mendeleev, provides a framework to organize the different elements that exist. For decades, teachers around the world have referred to this periodic table during chemistry classes. Regardless of where you grew up, you were exposed to this table at some point in your academic life.

During the tedious presentation, I fell into daydreaming mode.

What if I could give the periodic table of elements a new meaning? I wondered.

I began scribbling in my notebook. A sudden rush of energy took over. Bye-bye yawns — I was immersed in my creative thinking. Searching old memories, I could not recall what the periodic table looked like exactly, so out came the iPhone.

Using an image of the table for reference, I drew a series of small squares, organized in rows and columns. I was clearly not listening to the speaker anymore. Baseball has always been my passion, so I used the sport as a theme to fill every little square. I wrote the fundamental skills required to become a great player: swing mechanics, tracking fly balls, base running, throwing accuracy and so on.

Meanwhile, my co-author, Jean François (JF), was in Toronto, Canada, getting ready to give a keynote presentation to PepsiCo's upper management team. Moments before hopping on stage, his phone vibrated.

Incoming text message: André Lachance

As he had a few minutes to spare, he peeked at his phone to find out what I was up to. I'd sent him a text message containing no written information, only a picture of a bunch of squares filled with my hard-to-read handwriting. JF was confused.

I sent him a second text message: "We need to talk. I found something to structure our book. The periodic table of elements."

JF fired right back: "What are you talking about? You want to use a chemistry framework for our book? Are you out of your mind?! You know what I think about chemistry. Just thinking about that word makes me feel sick!" His text was followed by a green-faced emoji throwing up.

I texted JF back immediately: "Lol! We'll talk about it when I get back. I think you're going to like my idea."

Our relationship dates back to 2002. I'd taught a few coaching classes to JF during his Bachelors' Degree in Kinesiology at the University of Ottawa. At the time, I had just created Canada's first women's national baseball program and I was leading the charge as head coach. I was in the midst of getting the team ready to compete in two international tournaments. Young and green, JF was looking to join an elite sports program to gain some valuable experience, so one day after class, he approached me to share his interest in joining the team.

"Listen, if you need someone to help you do anything — write game summary reports, take stats, be your gofer, do whatever — I'm willing to help. I want to learn from you," he told me.

In class, I noticed the potential of the young student. His enthusiasm and eagerness to learn was palpable. A few days later, I called him up: "You're on board, kid! Get your passport ready. We're off to Japan this summer."

Who would have guessed that, 19 years later, we would become good friends and end up writing a book together? It was natural chemistry that brought us together.

When I returned to Canadian soil after my short trip to Cuba, I met up with JF to discuss the book.

"As you know, for the past few weeks, we've toyed around with many ideas to organize our concepts. None of them really stuck, right?"

JF agreed.

"Think about the periodic table of elements. Think of its utility. The framework serves to analyze and to explain chemical reactions, right?"

JF nodded.

I kept going, with enthusiasm. "From combining different elements, like H_2O for instance, you get molecules. What if we used a similar framework to organize our coaching concepts?"

JF thought it was original and sticky. He loved it.

Within seconds, we'd started brainstorming, writing different elements on Post-its and sticking them up on the wall. It only took an hour to come up with multiple elements. Near the end of the brainstorming session, JF suggested a title for the book.

"André, what if we called the book *Team Chemistry*? I mean, if we're going to use science-related terms, let's go all the way!"

"Yes!" I replied. "I'll be damned. Chemistry found a way to creep back into our lives!"

For centuries, it is through teamwork that humans battled in civil wars, created breakthrough inventions and survived international pandemics. In the sports realm, every success story is the result of collective efforts, where individuals come together to reach a common goal. Like the old adage says, alone you go fast, but together you go far.

The word "chemistry" is commonly used to explain the successes (sufficient chemistry) or failures (lack of chemistry) of sports teams.

But what is team chemistry, exactly?

Team chemistry is what happens when a group of individuals click and work well together. We are not alluding to teambuilding weekend getaways or singing "Kumbaya" together. It is much more complex than that. There are several elements to consider that influence team chemistry directly or indirectly, such as:

- robust coaching and leadership
- authentic mutual trust between teammates
- deep human connections
- effective communication, on and off the playing field
- a healthy team culture in the locker room
- caring about others around you
- positive team dynamics
- a common vision

The chapters in this book are written in a modular style, meaning you do not need to read a chapter to understand the next one. You can bounce freely from chapter 24, to 10, to 18, without getting lost. To offer some degree of organization to our periodic table of elements, we divided the book into four sections:

- Section 1: Creation
- Section 2: Communication

- Section 3: Collaboration
- Section 4: Coordination

Throughout these 30 chapters, we share practical tips to boost team chemistry in one way or another. Along the way, you will read anecdotes involving Lego, a Cirque du Soleil clown, a plane crash, a Greek mythology sculptor, a shooting in broad daylight and much more. Besides leadership skills, we also offer advice on managing situations that every coach will experience at some point in time, such as:

- cutting an athlete
- picking a coaching staff
- giving out awards
- having a difficult discussion
- managing a crisis

Our goal here is not to prescribe a formula of any kind. That is not our style. Instead, we just want to display a series of competencies, strategies and approaches that have served us well during our coaching careers. Choosing what made the cut for this book was no easy task. We chose content that coaches enjoy the most from our keynote speeches, classes, workshops and individual coaching sessions.

A few notes on style: The word "coach" will be used abundantly throughout this book to signify the leader of a team; however, in most cases, it can be replaced by another term that represents your performance environment better (e.g., manager, director, teacher, leader, mentor, etc.). As you navigate through the chapters, you will also notice the use of they/them pronouns unless we refer to a specific person or situation.

We took care to divide the writing of our book. You will be able to tell who wrote what based on our respective experiences and expertise that will be shared throughout the different chapters. I, André, am a baseball coach and university professor specializing in leadership training, team coaching and group efficacy. I built the first Women's National Baseball program in Canada and led the team as their coach for 15 years. If you see an anecdote involving coaching baseball, you'll know the chapter was written by me.

My co-author, JF, is a bestselling author and acclaimed mental performance expert who worked with Cirque du Soleil and has since coached multiple Olympic gold medallists, Super Bowl and X Games champions, NHL superstars, surgeons, pop stars and corporate leaders. When you read a story about an experience involving mental performance coaching, you'll recognize the writer as JF.

See this book like a restaurant buffet — focus on the chapters that ignite your tastebuds. Pick and choose the elements that are meaningful to your situation. Feel free to scribble, take notes and reflect on how you could adapt some of the book's advice to fit your coaching style.

SECTION 1

CREATION

**BUILDING A HEALTHY CULTURE,
LEARNING ABOUT THE TEAM AND
ESTABLISHING STRONG VALUES**

CHAPTER 1: KILOMETRE ZERO

If you have ever travelled to the large cities of Europe or other continents, perhaps you have noticed a small monument named "Kilometre Zero." This marker indicates the original point of a city, signifying the foundational stages of its establishment. At the time, Kilometre Zero served as the meeting point for people wanting to get together. The location also marked the starting point of all routes; hence the adage, "All roads lead to Rome." Thanks to the colonization of some areas in Latin America, you will find the same landmark in certain countries there. In Cuba, Kilometre Zero is located right near the El Capitolio building in Havana, next to a great café. Having studied in Havana at the Manuel Fajardo Sports Institute, I became familiar with this landmark.

Every team that has experienced success can look to its own Kilometre Zero. Usually, it is the anchor point from which a team culture will grow. This foundation will introduce the values and principles that, if properly demonstrated, will mould members of a group together. These standards must remain absolute and non-negotiable. They will help a team when it veers off course, falls into a slump or looks to resolve any in-house conflicts.

At their core, certain teams may feature such tenets as:

- effective communication
- respectful behaviour
- tireless work ethic
- excellence mindset
- courage and resilience

Some teams, like Liverpool FC, will even develop a manifesto, identifying in detail the principles that will guide their club operations. The key points of Liverpool's manifesto are the following:

- "You will never walk alone." There is a bond or kinship that all team members can rely on when the going gets tough.
- "We hold our heads high through the wind and the rain." Team members must never give up, no matter the circumstances or obstacles that may stand in their way.
- "We always give back." The team will be a presence in the community to help and support those in need.

Team culture grows from different roots and in many ways. Some clubs will be more expressive when showing their identity, while others may be more reserved. In all cases, a team's culture and the rules that come with it will form the group's DNA. This DNA can become the key to a team's success when the members of a team adhere to it without compromise.

When thinking of groups expressing their identity in a loud, exciting fashion, the New Zealand rugby team has to top the list. Even if you are not a fan of the sport, surely you have seen highlights of the national team's warm-up ritual. The haka is a ceremonial Maori dance performed by the players at mid-field, directly in front of their opponents. The tribal challenge consists of vigorous movements using the legs and arms, accompanied by loud chanting and intimidating looks. The haka has been a custom the New Zealand men's national rugby teams since 1905 and represents the perfect pre-game motivation for their warrior players. For the All Blacks, the haka is an opportunity to come together, connected in full harmony in preparation for a big game. It is a reminder that anything is possible when working as a unit. The haka is their Kilometre Zero. Everything else flows from that when playing a match.

Both JF and I have had the chance to visit Japan on a few occasions. Japanese culture is widely recognized for its respectful and polite nature. In Tokyo, for instance, you can leave your cell phone on a subway and, even after a long period of time, chances are you will find it in the exact spot you left it.

The courtesy displayed by Japanese people extends to the world of sports competition, to the envy of many coaches. For example, during the 2018 FIFA World Cup in Russia, the Japanese team was eliminated from the tournament with a devastating loss against Belgium, yet the defeated players still took the time to clean their dressing room. Soccer fans will remember the heartbreak of that match, one in which Japan held a two-goal advantage, only to fall 3–2. Nevertheless, the Japanese team members prepared a note, written in Russian, addressed to the tournament organizing committee and the people of Russia, thanking them for their gracious welcome during the competition. Respect being at the heart of their culture, this gesture was normal for the Japanese players and staff, even if perhaps considered extraordinary for many of us. To the Japanese, such principles take on far greater importance than the frustration and agony of defeat. Their Kilometre Zero even helps to soothe the sting when dealing with anguish.

A team's culture also affects the methods of scouting and selecting members of the team. Many sports leaders will choose their athletes partially based on how they identify with the club's culture. This was the case for France, soccer's world champion at the 2018 FIFA World Cup. During a conversation with one of the leaders of the national sport governing body, I quickly came to understand how French soccer scouts did not just observe technical skills and abilities when conducting roster recruitment. More precisely, officials also took into consideration such things as players' reactions to a bad coaching decision or a mistake by a teammate. If a player reacted poorly, their chances of making the team were reduced. This is an excellent reminder of how important applying team principles really is.

When formulating a team's DNA, coaches need to ask the following questions:

- What behaviour, practices and attitudes do I consider non-negotiable for our team?
- What will be the standards I set to establish our team's foundation and objective?

Below are some fundamental points to ponder to help you answer these questions.

DEVISE YOUR DNA WITH YOUR TEAM

It is very common for coaches and sports managers to create and impose their own culture instead of including group members when identifying performance and behavioural expectations. We do not suggest this. A culture formed by a group will have a better chance of thriving than one forced upon others by an individual.

To know
where to go,
you must first
know
where you are.

START WITH THE NON-NEGOTIABLES

It will be easier to obtain consensus from the beginning, which will provide momentum for developing any standards that follow. Feel free to use different language for these criteria, such as "absolutes" or "must-haves." "Show respect towards team personnel" is a good example of one of these rules. At no time should athletes demonstrate aggression or disrespect towards team coaches, staff or teammates, no matter what their decisions may be. Self-control among athletes must always be displayed.

MAKE IT RELEVANT

A culture should be shared, easy to understand and relatable. Create some visuals that provide reminders of the most important points. For our Canadian women's national baseball team, I developed (in collaboration with assistant coaches) 20 team standards. Here are some examples:

- Every practice is a good practice.
- Never let conflicts grow or linger.
- Always look someone in the eye when speaking with them.
- Be on time.
- Remember, we can face any situation or obstacle.

Bear in mind that during international competitions, athletes will need emphasis placed only on a handful of key expectations more fitting for that given moment. Coaches should choose what to emphasize based on the team's mindset and spirit at that specific time. These reminders can also trace back to meetings with athletes. Some coaches will even use these reminders during conflicts among team members.

KEEP UP WITH THE TIMES

Standards relating to team culture should be revisited regularly. Doing a check-in can help determine if anything should be tweaked, strengthened or removed based on the current roster and climate. Team members may leave while new ones arrive, so coaches should be prepared to modify the formula for a team's DNA.

CELEBRATE WHEN THE CULTURE WINS

Moments will occur when you realize culture played a strong role in a team having success. Be sure to use these times to further cement the value and importance of the culture as a pathway to that success. Highlight the displays that reinforce your Kilometre Zero. Celebrate your unique identity.

In recent years, we have had the opportunity to work with several large corporate enterprises. The culture developed within one of those Canadian corporations has made it one of the best in sales in the country. Not only that, but this company is also recognized as one of the top employers in North America on a regular basis. Looking at their DNA, we observe "curiosity," "inspiration" and "integrity" as the core of their decision-making and corporate objectives. These three elements combine individual and organizational performance so well — along with allowing for a perfect work–life balance — to reveal the company's Kilometre Zero. It is no surprise this company sits among the head of its class.

JF founded Kambio Performance Inc. with a very simple Kilometre Zero: "Surround yourself with good people." Everything stems from that. His consultants, partners, support staff and even clients are carefully chosen, based on Kilometre Zero. At the base, they are all qualified, but the quality of being a good person and having strong character will always count the most. This element of his company's DNA is non-negotiable. JF believes firmly that with good people, it is easy to deliver a good product. To date, this principle is entrenched and Kambio Performance continues to flourish year after year.

Time for reflection:

- What are your non-negotiables as the leader of your team?
- What are you not willing to compromise?
- What is your one principle that is the core of the team?
- Does your team have its own activity or thing that brings everyone together, like the haka?

We encourage you and your team to identify the fundamental values that will define your DNA. Kilometre Zero may not lead to Rome, but it will definitely lead to success in sports.

CHAPTER 2: BRAND

Think of a sports clothing brand. If Nike tops your list, count yourself among the majority. When we think of Nike, we think of the swoosh logo and of certain famous athletes associated with the company, like Serena Williams, LeBron James and Cristiano Ronaldo. The Nike brand remains popular today because it excels at communicating key pillars of performance, such as courage, determination and resilience. It is no wonder that the world's best athletes want the Nike name attached to theirs.

The same is the case for sports teams. For example, when we think of the NFL's Dallas Cowboys, the blue star on a silver helmet jumps out. While the symbol certainly is eye-catching, it represents so much more for the football team, the entire organization and the community. Not only is it a direct link to the state of Texas — the "Lone Star State" — but the star fills many with emotions of peace and serenity.

Your team's logo can help put you on centre stage. The goal in creating a logo is to ensure your brand stands out when compared to rival teams. The more your brand is recognized, the less your competitors will come to mind and the greater your athletes' exposure will be.

Decide what others say about you.

As the leader of your team, it is your job to find out what makes your program unique, both on and off the field. You also need to know as much as possible about your opponents, so take the necessary time to do your research. Does their behaviour, clothing or style of play set them apart from others? Having more information about your competition will put you in a good position to find the right elements to develop a unique image for your club.

There are many points to consider when establishing a successful brand. We invite you to take a closer look at how certain factors play a key role in creating a strong image.

THE NAME

You will probably inherit your team's name when you begin as coach. In many cases, the name of a team is chosen for reasons related to a city's culture or history. You may also have noticed that many teams use the name of animals who are fierce predators, like the Eagles, Lions or Coyotes. Clearly, being named the Tigers carries a far different connotation than being called the Rabbits. Predator or prey? The choice is easy.

As coach, you are encouraged to do some digging on the significance of your team's name. Take an interest in learning more about the meaning and values of your club identity. Many years ago, I found myself at the helm of a team named the Titans. Not knowing much about the name, I looked up some information on the internet and discovered that the Titans were the original gods in Greek mythology, giants who had come before the gods of Olympus. There were twelve of them altogether — six female, six male — and they were the sons and daughters of the sky and earth.

Certain words grabbed my attention: "giant" and "Olympus" denoted the sheer strength that represented the team. The word "earth" reminded us to keep our feet firmly planted on the ground and to always remain present. "Sky" encouraged the team to dare to dream. I used the number six regularly with my athletes when outlining important elements included in game strategies. By connecting more with those words, our brand and identity began reflecting the historical significance of our name.

Perhaps your team is called the Rebels, the Pirates or the Vikings. What can you learn about the significance of these names in order to enhance your team's brand?

THE COLOURS

If you are a basketball fan, you know the colour green is associated with the Boston Celtics. In baseball, when you think of pinstripes, you immediately think of the New York Yankees. The colours red, white and blue are commonly tied to the mystique of the NHL's legendary Montreal Canadiens.

The colour of a uniform can generate a sense of pride for an athlete. When an athlete feels proud, their identity will grow stronger. On the night of his number 33 jersey retirement ceremony, star hockey goaltender Patrick Roy shared these words with the adoring crowd paying him homage: "Tonight, we raise an important piece of my armour into the rafters. Yet, I will forever be proud to have worn the red, white and blue of the Montreal Canadiens."

Between 1940 and 2000, Cuba dominated the world baseball scene. They won 25 of the first 28 World Cups, 12 of 15 Pan American Games and 3 of 5 Olympic Games. Now *that* is what you call domination. The Cubans were known for wearing uniforms covered in red from head to toe, a stark contrast to the more conservative North American style featuring grey or white pants. Not only were their athletic talents superior, the Cubans appeared even stronger from just the colour of their uniforms. A game would not even start and the opponent would already be intimidated. A few years ago, Cuba altered its uniform, modernizing it and perhaps conforming to other countries' style; interestingly, the national team has suffered a setback in that same time. The country that ruled international baseball for decades has not been on top since the uniform change. Traditions are important for a team. While a team brand or image can adjust to keep up with present times, if it abandons or neglects its roots, negative effects can surface.

What do your team colours signify? Does green call to mind the forces of nature, or silver the courage of knights? Try putting this challenge to your team members and see how they respond when determining the value of your team colours in order to give your brand more weight.

THE SLOGAN

"Just do it." "Think different." "I'm lovin' it." Even with time, our brain still registers Nike, Apple and McDonald's as the companies behind these slogans. These short and catchy phrases have not only become embedded in our minds but have also encouraged a similar practice in non-business environments. Consider these examples from various sports:

- Toronto Raptors (NBA): *We the North*
- Detroit Red Wings (NHL): *Hockeytown: No limits.*
- Liverpool FC (Premier League): *You'll Never Walk Alone.*
- Los Angeles Dodgers (MLB): *Live. Breathe. Blue.*

Your team's slogan must align with the team's fundamental principles so it resonates with all of your team members. This is an ideal opportunity for a coach to connect a team's history with their coaching philosophy. (See chapter 1, "Kilometre Zero," for more details.)

Choosing a slogan also provides a unique opportunity to cement a critical thought in the minds of your team members. With our women's national baseball team, I once created a video that included the slogan "Be One," reinforcing the importance of standing united in order to obtain our goals. For me, short slogans have always stood out. They are far easier to remember and be repeated within a group.

Remember, athletes are always seeking belonging and affiliation. With a strong slogan, you can solidify your organizational image while also bolstering your team chemistry.

THE RITUALS

Following his many wins at world championships and the Olympic Games, Usain Bolt, also known as the fastest man alive, would perform a victory celebration move that would become his image. The "lightning bolt" quickly went viral and many people have used it since. Bolt's ritual has definitely become a part of his brand.

Rituals have been around for ages and the most common example in team sports is the rally cry. This gathering together of players serves as a unifying activity and can encourage one another during a crucial point in a game. The practice can also inspire and motivate teams when used as a pre-game and post-game custom. With some teams in the past, I would use the rally cry to help players forget trivial parts of daily life and connect to the team and our objective. Following games, our team cheer signalled a time to unplug and return to the realities of life outside our sport.

During international competitions, the national anthem is part of the pre-game ritual. I was reflecting on this one day, wondering if we could use our anthem to better unite our team while showing our strength to our opponents. The next season during a training session in Cuba, I assembled our athletes into a conference room at our hotel.

"All right, everyone. Tonight, we will be practising our routine during the national anthems."

The players all looked at me with confusion. I reminded them that this moment represented the first impression our opponent and the fans would have of us. We all lined up, standing next to each other. These were my instructions:

1. Hold your ball cap with your right hand and along your body during the other country's national anthem.
2. With the right hand, hold your ball cap across your chest during our country's anthem.
3. At all times, keep your body posture straight with your head facing the flag.
4. When the final note has played, count three seconds in your head before placing your ball cap on your heads in unison and run back to the dugout.

When we did this that night, our team body language was perfectly synchronized. The message was clear: from the playing of the national anthems, Canada was ready and we came to play. Players and coaches from other teams later approached me, saying any game against Canada was always a tough matchup and they knew nothing would come easily. Our message had been received.

No matter what your ritual may be, remember it should unify your team. This team tradition is important to the players and should not be dismissed or ignored. What ritual can you introduce to help your team stand out? How can your image be different from all other teams?

Your team brand will have an effect on your athletes and staff — positive or negative. As humans, we hate rejection while we crave belonging and seek a positive sense of identity. A successful brand can help your team in the following ways:

- With greater engagement and commitment at all levels, your players will want to leave a positive mark on the team's history.
- Fostering feelings of belonging results in players having an increased willingness to continue improving, which prompts a better effort.
- A higher level of satisfaction — your athletes will feel pride and have fun when involved in creating a team brand.
- Your roster will have a lower turnover rate because players will not want to leave the team if they feel emotionally attached to the group.
- When players bond together, they will carry it into competition, support one another and experience better results.

Whatever it is, your team image will stick with you. You will choose how to define it and display it. To help do this, you can mount plaques or signs in your locker room, have T-shirts made featuring important team messages or use social media posts to broadcast your #brand via the internet.

Remember, if you do not control your team image and reputation, be assured your competitors will do that for you. What do you want others to say about you? It is your call.

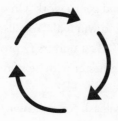

CHAPTER 3: TEAM CYCLES

A sports team will go through different stages over time. If you take a closer look, you'll find the stages are quite similar to the cycle of life.

It all starts when a new team comes to life. Everyone is open-minded and eager to get started. Then comes the growing pains (childhood) and the identity crisis (adolescence). Not long after follows adulthood, when valuable wisdom starts emerging, before the team finally enters the old age stage where life is less stressful and more free flowing. But as with every cycle, the journey must come to an end at some point.

In this chapter, we break down the cycle into different phases. For each phase, we offer contextual details to describe their traits before offering strategies to better manage the challenges that occur within each phase.

BIRTH

Welcome. You have just taken over a team. Some athletes are veteran players while a few others are newcomers. You are thrilled to meet your new crew and get to work. On paper, it seems like the team has the potential to win it all. You also feel that you are the right leader for the job. As a university professor, I get the same feeling when I start a semester with new students.

Excitement is in the air!

At this stage, you will ask yourself many questions:

- What will be the identity of this group?
- Who should be in the starting lineup?
- How many personalities will be tough to handle?
- Will I be able to make this team grow to their full potential?

While questions fire off in your mind, athletes will have inquiries of their own:

- Who is this coach?
- What will they have to offer?
- How will I develop under their leadership?
- What will be their style? Authoritarian? Laissez-faire?

When humans are born, they do not choose the family they grow up in. They do not decide who the parents and siblings are, nor do they choose the environment in which they are raised. It is no different in a sports context. Most of the time, athletes end up on a team and have no control over who will coach them, who their teammates will be or what the team setting will look like.

During this phase, the primary goal is for the athletes and coaches to learn about each other and get along. Usually, things run relatively smooth as everyone tends to be nice and polite with each other. On the other hand, it is at this time first impressions are made and athletes can be quick to judge someone else on the team. (See chapter 8, "Pygmalion," for more details.)

Keep in mind that athletes are looking for direction from their coach during this early phase.

Strategies to Manage this Stage

Now is the time for team activities that can help the athletes discover the different personalities on the team. Sports-related or not, choose team building activities that will expose athletes' characters. Small cliques might start emerging and that is fine.

It is common during the birth phase for athletes to repeatedly ask questions. Be patient and offer answers to their inquiries. This is also a good time to come up with team rules, values and a code of conduct.

You may have found yourself in a situation where you have become your child's coach. This situation may result in you spending less time interacting with the other athletes on the team. Take advantage of the situation and assign your child to another coach on the team. Children tend to listen more to feedback from a coach who is not their parent. This is also a good time to get to know parents, involve them in practices and make sure communication is clear in regard to what is expected of their child. This investment will pay off later.

In the early stages of a team, I encourage coaches to be firm and strict by using a directive style of coaching. I experienced an interesting birth-stage moment during my very first season with the national baseball team. I had introduced some simple team rules: athletes must wear the black jersey during warm-up and the red (or white) jersey for the game. Easy rules to follow, right?

While the players started warming up for the first game of a World Cup tournament, I noticed that one of our best players was wearing red instead of black. I asked her to come over. I could hear the other coaches whispering, probably wondering how I was going to manage the star player.

"The team rule is black jersey for warm-ups, you know that, right?"

"Yes, I know, but I forgot it at the hotel."

"So, if you don't have your black jersey, you can't do the warm-up, correct?"

"Uh, I guess so . . ."

"And if you can't warm up, well then you can't play, right?"

"Uh . . . well . . . I guess . . ."

"So according to the team rules, you're not playing today. Sorry."

I chose a directive style to respect the rules. If I had made an exception and let it slide this one time, I might have lost control of the team. As a result, I chose to be firm despite knowing that she would be angry about the decision.

And angry she was. But, from that moment on, she kept reminding other players to pack their black jersey so that no one else would experience the same fate. This episode happened back in 2004 and players on the current national team who have never met the player are still talking about it.

The black jersey rule has been followed ever since.

ADOLESCENCE

Ah, the teenage years. A time of confusion, discoveries, identity searching and clumsiness. During this phase, adolescents want to fit in, to make their presence felt and to do everything their own way. Arguing and disagreeing seem to be the preferred pastimes — it's a challenging time for parents.

Sports teams also go through this rebellious phase. Coaches start to see the real personalities come out. All of a sudden, the politeness and respectfulness from the birth stage starts to fade away. Instead, a series of conflicts begin to emerge . . . and they must be resolved before it is too late. The coach's authority usually gets tested. The naysayers wake up. Frustration sets in, and sometimes successful performances are hard to come by. You will start seeing strong cliques forming and big personalities storming.

I remember asking myself if I would ever get through this stage with some former teams:

- Do I have the right skills to manage this situation?
- How long will this crisis last?
- Will I get through this?
- Did I make a mistake taking this team on?
- Why is this happening to me?

This is the make-or-break stage — you must resolve the growing pains or the team's progression will suffer for a long time.

In the mid-1990s, I was coaching two different sports. My summers were devoted to baseball and the winter months were spent in gymnasiums coaching badminton. I faced my first teenage crisis with a badminton player while coaching at Laval University. During a practice, a player challenged me in front of everyone.

"What's the point of this drill, anyway? Why are we doing it today? Why not do it tomorrow or next week?"

I had never been confronted that way before. As a young and inexperienced coach, all I could say was "Because . . . uh . . . ," without any further information. What a mistake. I must say, that was one of the most unforgettable moments, for negative reasons, of my coaching career. However, I learned a great lesson.

During the next training session, the same athlete challenged me again. This time, I was prepared. With robust confidence, I peppered back with concise, short and direct answers. "This drill is important because it will help you get out of vulnerable positions. Your position will be better on the court, which could get you back on top in the rallies. You will be harder to beat."

She never challenged me again. Since then, I have made it my duty to prepare fully for training, making sure to have a specific purpose behind every drill, not only to optimize the training but so I can explain to athletes how each activity links to competition.

Strategies to Manage this Stage

During this phase, if you see some light at the end of the tunnel after dealing with a difficult situation, beware, because that light might be a high-speed train coming right at you. During this teenage phase, when a problem is solved, chances are it will show up again in the future. Do not take anything for granted.

I suggest keeping any debating and negotiating with athletes short and sweet, like I did with the badminton player. If athletes are on edge, no need to add fuel to the fire. Do not go down that road. If ever the team wants to modify a team rule, like extending curfew time, it might be strategic to cooperate and accept the compromise. See it as brownie points for the future.

I have realized that focusing on taking care of team goals rather than trying to fix every interpersonal issue in your group, which might be mission impossible, is time well spent during the adolescent phase.

When coaching younger athletes, this stage may come sooner than you think. For example, you may get emails from parents, early in the season, complaining that their child isn't playing enough. Resist the temptation to go back and forth with emails, trying to justify and explain the situation. This process may never end. Instead, schedule a meeting to talk it out and address the situation, like before or after a practice.

The coach must also find out who the most influential personalities in the group are. Getting your message across is not always easy and these athletes have power — they can help make your message stick with the team. You can identify the leaders easily by using a sociogram. (See chapter 16, "Sociogram," for more details.)

EARLY ADULTHOOD

After the challenging teenage years comes early adulthood, a period of life when people complete their studies, start their first serious job, seek financial stability and start an independent lifestyle. Non-essential conflicts are a thing of the past and people are ready to move on to more serious endeavours.

This transition from immature conduct to more mature behaviour also happens within the development of a team. All of a sudden, team members start appreciating each other much more. Different and divergent opinions become less distracting. Instead, athletes are more interested in working together to reach a common goal. Team chemistry starts to emerge.

Typically, the leader's credibility and authority are no longer questioned, or at least not nearly as much as during the adolescence stage.

You will also witness athletes getting more comfortable with staff members. They reach out more for help when needed. The roles and responsibilities are better defined, which increases team efficiency and creates a friendlier environment for athletes.

Strategies to Manage this Stage

This stage is a refreshing change. Things are finally rolling; however, it is imperative that the coach keeps an eye out for any behaviours that could derail the train and make it go back to the previous adolescent stage. It took so much work to finally get here, you do not want to see it go to waste.

Make sure to offer positive reinforcement while remaining direct and unapologetic, to show that you acknowledge their efforts. You are at a point where asking athletes questions during meetings is safe. The mutual trust is strong enough for deeper team conversations. Encourage shy individuals to participate as well.

Team conversations are more open now, so your role as a facilitator is vital. Managing discussions so that every individual has a voice is key for team decisions. It is also perfect timing to give away responsibilities, like letting the athletes choose the restaurant for the next team dinner.

During this phase, I would let the athletes choose which uniforms to wear for games. Several combinations were possible — white/grey pants, black/red/grey jerseys and black/red/white caps. Handing over some control to the athletes can strengthen the team bond.

You can also consider creating a small leadership group within the team: for example, three experienced athletes could share observations from a past performance that could influence your tactics for an upcoming match against the same opponent. (See chapter 19, "Inner Teams," for more ideas.)

ADULTHOOD

When we reach adulthood, we are finally mature enough to know our wants and needs. People are more confident at work. Couples start families. Life is more stable, responsibilities are abundant and people offer their best self to others.

When your team reaches adulthood, things are usually rolling. Collectively, athletes believe in the system and are looking forward confidently. Everyone is motivated, working hard and pushing in the same direction. Great achievements, like winning championships, only happen in this phase. The team is tapping into its full potential.

Players are leaving their egos at the door for the benefit of the team. Collective support is strong, making the environment safe and conducive to high performance.

Mutual trust is so strong that you feel totally confident delegating responsibilities to others. As a result, others around you respect you even more.

Strategies to Manage this Stage

In this stage, coaches do not dictate as much as they did in the past. Instead, the coach acts primarily as an advisor and a guide. It is important to first make the athletes question their own objectives and then direct them down the right path. Coaches are not teaching new content so much anymore; the job is more about offering cues and reminders.

While it is essential to offer some slack during this phase, you must still remain on the lookout for distractions and detractors who might try to wreck the ship. For example, gossips, controversial journalists or the odd bad apple on the team.

Also, consider the potential that assistant coaches have on the team. Perhaps they are ready for new challenges, like taking on more responsibilities or even getting a shot as head coach for another team.

THE END

Timewise, this stage deserves some attention, as every team journey comes to an end at some point, whether it's the end of an Olympic cycle or the end of a season. No one can escape it. These are emotional times as much for those who leave as for those who stay. The team must adapt to the changes, for better or worse.

Strategies to Manage this Stage

At this point, the coach must reassure the athletes by explaining what lies ahead. You must show empathy for those who have trouble letting go or those who resist change. The timing is right to celebrate individual contributions and team accomplishments.

For the coach, the end stage is a time of self-reflection as the leader of the team:

- What did I learn from this team?
- What will I do differently with the next team?
- Are any older athletes who are preparing for life after sports interested in staying with the team, like becoming a coach or an administrator?

It is common for coaches to put lots of thought and effort into getting the team up and running at the beginning of a team cycle and then give less importance to the ending, but the last moments experienced in a team are often the ones athletes remember the most. Make sure to conclude the journey on a positive note.

Understanding the team cycle is critical for any coach. You will notice which stage your team is in by paying attention to how the athletes are interacting and behaving. Then, you can adapt how you intervene and choose the correct leadership style accordingly.

Where's
your
team
at?

CHAPTER 4: STAFF

At the Formula One Brazilian Grand Prix in 2019, the Aston Martin Red Bull Racing Team and its driver Max Verstappen were getting prepared to clock the fastest time over 71 laps. When everything was in place, the lights lit up to give drivers the starting signal.

At the 21st lap, it was time for Max to pull off for a pit stop. Upon his arrival, the crew members were in position, knowing exactly what their roles were and how to execute them. They had practised this drill hundreds of times to keep the pit stop as short as possible. Each member had specific responsibilities: lifting the racecar, removing the lug nuts and worn tires, mounting the new tires on the car, refastening the lug nuts, lowering the car back down and stepping back as the car takes off again. Truly a perfectly synchronized choreography, right to a T.

The average time for changing four tires during a Formula One pit stop is 2.4 seconds. In a sport where a fraction of a second can determine finishing in first or second place, a fast pit stop can make all the difference.

Thanks to exceptional teamwork, the Aston Martin Red Bull Racing Team's pit crew completed the stop in . . . 1.82 seconds!

Not only did they break their own record, they also made history by setting a new Guinness World Record for the fastest pit stop in Formula One racing history. Imagine changing a flat tire on the side of the highway, mounting your spare wheel after just experiencing a tire puncture. Considering this picture, it would seem impossible to imagine how a group can execute this task so quickly.

As team manager or head coach, you will likely need to choose assistants and support staff that will help you in leading the program. Bringing in the right people is critical. Your hiring selections could include assistant coaches, trainers, a mental performance coach, a nutritionist, a physiotherapist and others. This is your Integrated Support Team (IST). The goal of the IST will be to serve as the engine that drives the car — or team, in this case — as fast and as far as possible, obtaining maximum performance and optimal efficiency.

Choosing your staff is a process never to be taken lightly. Your group could be working together the entire year, so a meticulous approach is required. Here are some strategies that can help you in choosing the right staff and making sure their roles are clear.

QUALITY VS. QUANTITY

For many teams, the first instinct is to think more staff equals more success. In theory, this could translate to hiring specialists of all sorts. This is often the case with sports teams or programs blessed with big budgets. You must always be cautious, however, since the greater the staff number, the greater the need for staff management.

Let's take communication as an example. As head coach, you will need to oversee many channels of communication. If your support staff consists of six individuals, it creates 15 possible communication routes. Add two members to your staff and you will take on 13 new communication avenues. It is good to keep this in

Your staff
should
complete you,
not
resemble you.

mind, as the more staff we hire, the more challenging the communication, and the more likely it can go wrong.

Another issue with having a big staff is the possibility of having too many different philosophies or approaches. While variety can be an asset, a larger staff size can present a risk of too many differing opinions, possibly leading to unnecessary conflict.

The Verstappen pit crew includes 19 members — no more, no less. This exact number is set for one reason only: to ensure maximum efficiency during pit stops. If the group were smaller, times could run longer since certain tasks would not finish as quickly. Conversely, too many people around the racecar would take up more space, making movement more difficult. It is the same for coaches. To optimize your staff and team's overall performance, always focus on quality and not quantity.

So how many staff should you have for an ideal number in your crew?

POINT OF CONTACT

No matter how many people you take on board, you must also consider who will have direct access to the team. The idea here is to limit the number of different voices that will address the team throughout the year. This will help reduce the number of obstacles that can arise when messages are delivered to athletes.

For example, if we had specific instructions to give the baseball players regarding their plate appearances during our team meetings, only the hitting coach would talk to the team. This coach's expertise is hitting, so they should be the players' single point of contact when they have any questions or concerns related to the subject. Sometimes a head coach, wanting to control everything, steps in and speaks up, offering mixed messages to the athletes. This nasty habit could create problems. For the players' sake, it is far more efficient to employ the KISS philosophy (keep it simple, silly). After all, too many cooks in the kitchen can ruin the recipe.

On a Formula One team, the main resource for the driver during a race is the crew chief. The rest of the team have their microphones off and can only listen to radio contact, in order to not distract the driver. In a sport like auto racing, the smallest bit of disruption can prove to be distracting or even fatal for the person behind the wheel.

PROTECTING YOUR EGO

Many coaches make the mistake of choosing their staff members based strictly on their personalities. In fact, they will appoint assistant coaches who reflect their philosophy and who will largely support their decisions. Surely, you can think of a few examples when you've seen this happen.

Why do coaches do this? Because at their core, they are afraid of having their ego bruised or their authority challenged. This is one clear hindrance to personal development.

Early in my coaching days, I made the mistake of surrounding myself with people I got along well with, both on and off the field. I figured it would be easier that way. While we may have had our fair share of success, I certainly limited my opportunity to become a better coach. I missed the chance to become vulnerable to individuals who could have challenged my tactics and taught me new approaches.

When in the position of leader, we must always remember our primary objective is to make our team better and gain the greatest success. If the coach can improve their own abilities, the whole team will benefit. When selecting your athletes, would you choose individuals who all display the same assets, playing style and personality? Of course not. The same should hold true, then, when forming your staff.

A Formula One team is made up of individuals that have talents and skills completely different from one another. They are not competing against each other; instead, each member is looking to complement the other. Accepting and appreciating everyone's roles will enhance the team's success and potentially set the table for a pit stop in under two seconds.

Even if everyone has their own job to do, there will be times when another member of the staff can provide valuable help for the head coach. So put your ego aside and welcome those opportunities as a chance to grow.

TERRITORY

The majority of conflicts within a coaching group occur when a member of the staff crosses responsibility lines or breaks from an established role. It is a question of territory. For example, the mental performance coach would be responsible for athletes' concentration, motivation and confidence, while the strength and conditioning coach is in charge of their physical strength and speed training. If both coaches stay within their lane, there should be no problems.

If only it were that simple.

As some athletes will develop a stronger connection with certain members of staff, stepping outside defined roles is almost inevitable. Boundaries are not always clearly defined. Staff members must always respect each other's duties but there should also be flexibility when necessary. In all cases, when an individual steps out of their specified area of responsibility, they should discuss the situation with all affected staff members in order to avoid any conflicts that could follow. There is nothing worse than a secret revealed too late.

As a baseball head coach, I once had to assist both technically and tactically with a pitcher. Before doing anything else, I wanted to speak with our pitching coach in order to ensure my comments and suggestions to the player would align with his philosophy and established strategies.

Returning to our Formula One friends, just as a task may be very specific and require a certain level of collaboration, no one should ever interfere in the business of someone else. It will be up to you to determine what a given situation calls for to develop a synergy that will advance your team.

CURIOSITY

Successful teams often stand out due to their continuous innovation and creativity. To stay at the top of their sport, the Formula One stables are always seeking to reinvent themselves. Engineers are constantly researching and developing new technologies to improve a car and the driver's performance. For example, technology such as virtual simulators for driver training and the continual modifications to a car's design to make it more aerodynamic.

As curiosity lies at the heart of innovation, I am always looking for individuals with inquisitive minds to help me improve my coaching and our team. This curiosity intensifies when we ask questions that will deepen our critical thinking and provoke further reflection. With intention and respect, we can continually grow our team's spirit. In the end, our crew will be more effective and we will boost our creativity while comfortably managing any changes that may come.

An open mind should remain the central part of any strategy when recruiting staff. If you like the idea of your team moving faster or obtaining results that exceed expectations, a prudent selection process for naming coaches and support staff members is as important as choosing players for your roster. You may never change a car tire in 1.82 seconds, but you can accelerate the development of your sports program.

CHAPTER 5: WELCOME

In recent years, different movements such as #MeToo and Black Lives Matter have heightened social awareness. Coaches must make efforts to create a more inclusive environment. While this has proven relatively easy for some, it has been very difficult for others. Yet, we must remind ourselves sports have always provided an extraordinary platform for showing others a good example. As head coach, your actions can have great impact and you must never underestimate this. Your words and your deeds can influence so many lives, positively or negatively.

While working with Cirque du Soleil, I met a female gymnast who had struggled with bulimia since the age of 13. In asking her a few questions, I came to understand that her eating disorder had begun eight years earlier as a result of a comment made by her coach, who told her she was fat. An exchange lasting mere seconds caused many years of psychological and physical distress. Some words certainly are heavy.

When writing this chapter, I recalled my own experiences as an athlete. I asked myself how my coaches acted when I was a young hockey player. For decades, the sport has been like a religion in Canada. Unfortunately, because of its macho culture, disrespectful behaviours have often been accepted and tolerated without anyone taking notice or action. I reflected upon how my coaches would frequently use vulgar and inappropriate language. Expressions and comments were often racist, sexist or discriminatory. Since the coach was seen as an authority figure, no one dared point out his wrongful behaviour. While some athletes may have found his comments funny, many others, including myself, found them extremely out of line. The coach's inappropriate language divided the team.

We hope you are not this type of coach, but perhaps you have witnessed similar actions or comments. It's important to be mindful of your words and actions, especially in the presence of your athletes and team community.

To ensure a strong and healthy team chemistry, members must feel welcomed, comfortable and well-received in the group. Why? It is simple: nobody likes rejection. (See chapter II, "P.R.P" for more details.) Athletes are no exception. They, too, want to be included and feel they are part of the family. It is a core need for us as humans. The feeling of being rejected lies at the heart of abandonment for certain athletes who later turn to other pursuits where their differences will not be brushed aside. This is why a coach plays such an important role in creating an atmosphere where each member feels comfortable and accepted as part of the group.

To help stir some reflection, let's look at a series of examples that show common coaching actions and some alternative behaviours.

EXPRESSIONS

Humans are creatures of habit. Expressions used in the past are often so entrenched in the brain that the idea of adopting a different communication strategy can be difficult for some coaches. But we all have to make an effort to unlearn mental anchors weighing us down. Here are some common examples of this:

All right guys, listen up! While there may be no bad intention behind the use of the word "guys," certain members in a group may not identify with this gendered term. Instead, you can try words like "team," "everybody," "group," "gang" or another non-gendered term that can apply to everyone.

You're my athlete; My team played well yesterday; You didn't do what I asked of you; Give me three more laps. These expressions carry a possessive connotation. They are controlling and dominating, implying the athlete is your personal property. No individual belongs to another. Furthermore, such phrases can reinforce the belief that the coach is more important than the team or athletes. Here are some more appropriate alternatives: "You are an athlete that I train."; "The team that I coach played well yesterday."; "You didn't do what we agreed to."; and "Please run three more laps."

Girls are more sensitive than boys; Boys are stronger than girls. No matter what your thoughts or intentions are, think again. Some situations call for sensitivity, while others require strength and neither is specifically linked to gender.

He is Black, so he must be physically stronger than the others. In this case, the coach is clearly biased and is using skin colour as a determining factor for athletic performance. Physical appearance alone is certainly no guarantee for athleticism.

Sit down in Indian position, please. Despite being an expression used for decades, this is an unacceptable statement. Instead, ask your athletes to sit with their legs crossed.

Girls who play team sports are lesbians. This is a prejudiced statement. Sexual orientation has no bearing on an athlete's abilities and the best team cultures are diverse and inclusive. Denying an athlete the opportunity to compete because of sexual orientation is discriminatory and serves only to diminish sport.

You're crazy; That was sick. Avoid these expressions at all costs. Often used to describe an extraordinary performance, the words "crazy" and "sick" are also closely linked to mental health. Other expressions are far more suitable, such as "Wow, what a performance!"; "You were so courageous!"; and "You're a powerhouse."

Let's have girls on this side and guys on the other. With this instruction, a coach limits an individual's choice to identify between the two traditional genders. Many other options exist when you need to split a group for an activity. For example, you can assign a number system like ones and twos, or organize by day or month of birth, to achieve your goal.

Tell your mom to please be on time for the meeting. What if the player has no parents or has two fathers or two mothers? Never take anything for granted. For this reason, it is wise to use words like "parent," "guardian" or "caregiver."

You throw like a girl; Let go of your purse; Get rid of your skirt. Today, coaches still use female-gendered words to describe a weak performance, especially within male sports. There is no need to associate a poorly executed skill with girls or women. A weak performance is simply a weak performance, period. So please, just say it as it is.

These are just some examples. You can probably come up with many others from your experiences in sports and day-to-day life.

What happens if a member of your team uses an inappropriate term or expression? Each person, including the head coach, should be aware of their language, but no one is perfect and such occurrences can take place. These are golden opportunities for the coach to show leadership and address any offensive language. It is important not to ignore or downplay the situation, particularly when dealing with exclusionary language. Otherwise, unacceptable words and actions can become commonplace and this can lead to greater problems for the team. Always be sure to remain aware of your team's culture and monitor behaviour among players and staff. We encourage teams to develop a zero-tolerance policy with appropriate associated consequences, forbidding any speech or practice that rejects or neglects any team member.

It is also important that your team members feel supported. Encouraging your group to inform you if your comments offend them can go a long way in maintaining a respectful environment. This can also help refine your choice of words in important communication moments.

PLAYER NAMES

Imagine a coach reading off the list of players. He notices that almost all the first names are common and from his own cultural background, but one jumps off the page. He lifts his eyes from his clipboard, looks around in front of him and sees that every player is white except for one. The coach approaches the boy to introduce himself and shake hands: "Hi there, and welcome to the team. You must be Youssef."

When presented with a name we do not recognize, our brain has a tendency to quickly associate it with another culture. The coach in the situation above presumes this is the case when he instantly identifies the player with a different skin colour. Be careful not to make assumptions, however, as this can prove to be inappropriate, embarrassing and even hurtful for an individual.

To avoid an uncomfortable exchange like this, you can ask for players' names when introducing yourself. For example:

"Hi, I'm Jean François and I'll be your coach. What's your name?"

Make the
athletes
feel
at home.

When working with a name that might be difficult to pronounce, always ask the player to help staff and players say it properly. Most definitely, a coach should avoid giving a player a nickname in order to prevent having to learn the player's actual name. I recall witnessing a coach who nicknamed a player of Chinese background "Ching" during an introduction at an early practice. The coach addressed the player this way all season. You could even forgo the nickname option on the team entirely. While nicknames often bring a deeper intimacy and familiarity to your group, not all individuals enjoy the practice, especially if they didn't select their nickname.

TONE OF VOICE

It is the start of a new season. You are anxious to meet the athletes on your team. Some are returning for a second or third season, but you also have many others you do not already know as part of the squad. As the players arrive, you greet the familiar faces with enthusiasm.

"Hey! How was your summer? I'm happy to see you. How are your parents doing? It's great to have you back with the team."

You then approach a new player you have not coached before. Your tone changes and you bluntly offer, "Good afternoon. How are you? We'll be starting our training session soon."

The difference here is clearly in your approach. Remember, the new players are seeking a connection with the coach just as much as the returning ones, maybe even more so because they are adjusting to an environment that is new to them. It is your responsibility to ensure everyone feels welcome and that all newcomers' initial experiences are as pleasant as possible. Be sure to adjust your speaking tone so that it remains the same from one player to the next.

INDIVIDUAL DIFFERENCES

Especially for younger kids, it is not uncommon for sports teams to have a ritual of eating a snack after a game. Snack time usually features a juice box, a granola bar or a tasty treat like an ice cream sandwich. However, in addition to individual players' specific dietary practices, some cultures observe specific food restrictions. While a team snack can be an excellent idea, the tradition can turn out to be embarrassing or uncomfortable for any athlete who cannot take part. It is always good to check with the parents or players themselves at the start of the year to confirm any food allergies or other restrictions.

The same applies for holidays. "Merry Christmas, everyone!" may not carry the same meaning for all. "Have a great holiday, everybody!" can show a more inclusive wish.

We would like to share some insights from Vanessa Riopel, a former athlete André coached for seven years as part of the Canadian women's national baseball team. She explained to us how her experience and the national team environment helped her in her personal life.

"From my first days with the team, I felt André was genuinely interested in getting to know me and learning more about my life in general. During one of our early conversations, he asked me if I had a partner in my life — a boyfriend or a girlfriend. For the first time, a person asked about someone other than a boyfriend. This really struck me. At a time when my sexual orientation was still a bit of a secret, I was always excited to return to the national team each summer, since my teammates' and coaches' support made me feel so good. There's not a doubt in my mind that I wouldn't have the life I have today, with my girlfriend and three children, were it not for our team and its welcoming and inclusive environment."

As a coach, if you can succeed in creating an environment where the Vanessas on your team feel welcomed and supported, imagine the impact you can have on your team's performance.

CHAPTER 6: OOPS

Syphilis was very common in Europe during the 18th and 19th centuries. This sexually transmitted infection was primarily passed on through unprotected sex. Using protection was uncommon at the time, so other measures were needed to prevent the virus from spreading. German scientist Paul Ehrlich began working on a cure for the deadly disease.

After countless hours of trial and error, Ehrlich finally found that cure in 1909. During a press conference that announced the great news to the world, a journalist asked the scientist what the name of the remedy was. After hesitating for a brief moment, the German answered, "606." Confused, the press inquired about the unusual name. The inventor mentioned that it had taken 606 attempts to figure out the cure.

"I failed 605 times. But the 606th was the right one. I can't think of a better name."

Thanks to his acceptance of his mistakes, he persevered and made a Nobel Prize–worthy discovery that ended up saving thousands of lives.

Discoveries like Ehrlich's happen because "Oops" moments are accepted as part of the process. He never got discouraged. He gave himself permission to fail. Ask yourself the following:

- As the leader of my team, do I give myself the permission to fail?
- Is my coaching staff allowed to make big mistakes?
- Are athletes able to trip and fall without getting reprimanded?

Before going further, I want to make something clear: when undertaking any challenge that pushes your team's limits, difficulties and setbacks will stand in the way. Do not act surprised when they show up. You must expect and welcome them.

As a mental performance coach, I love telling athletes, "If you never fail, it doesn't make you perfect, it just means what you are doing is not hard enough!"

Making mistakes is part of the process, especially when your team is looking to reach another level or accomplish something new, like becoming champions for the first time. Consider why an eraser is attached to the end of a pencil. Have you ever gone through an entire lead pencil without using the eraser? Of course not.

Great discoveries, successful business stories and historical sport achievements all have a common theme: failure before success. Thomas Edison, famously known for inventing the light bulb, experienced thousands of Oops moments. Bill Gates's first business went bankrupt. The Wright brothers needed numerous attempts before their plane lifted off the ground. Walt Disney dealt with bankruptcy before creating his empire. Oops, oops and oops. There are so many examples: tech giant Steve Jobs, music legends The Beatles, writer J.K. Rowling, scientist Albert Einstein, superstar athlete Michael Jordan and former president Abraham

Lincoln. They experienced Oops moments to foster personal growth, which ultimately led to overwhelming success.

Oops moments were frequent when I was a kid. When I learned to walk, to swim, to pedal a bike, to count and to read, my parents were my coaches and were always close by, cheering me on. They ignored my failed attempts and encouraged me to keep going.

Once we become adults, most of us develop an unhealthy relationship with failure, as if we are not allowed to make any mistakes. In my case, looking back, the academic system probably did not help: As a student, I was penalized for making mistakes. I used to dread seeing the red ink on tests and papers I wrote. Naturally, my intentions were conditioned to avoid mistakes at all costs.

The limbic system does not help either. Also called the reptilian brain, this area in our brain has one goal: to ensure human survival by protecting us from any threats. So, when we associate a mistake with being in trouble or feeling worthless, we become panicky and want to flee the moment to avoid discomfort and vulnerability.

Let me give you an example.

Most Cirque du Soleil performers partake in specialized courses before joining a show. The artists perfect their skills through a series of classes, like clown training, for example. For gymnasts with limited artistic abilities, these sessions force them to step out of their comfort zones. Feeling vulnerable and uncomfortable during these classes is perfectly normal. Show managers do not expect the newcomers to become expert artists from the beginning; they are aware that the learning curve for some artists will take several weeks. For former athletes, like gymnasts, who were accustomed to competing in front of judges, making a fool out of themselves was not something they particularly enjoyed or were accustomed to doing. Plus, it had been ages since these acrobats were beginners at a given task, which was an ideal setup to put their limbic system in overdrive.

To help the artists deal with the feeling of discomfort, and to also avoid sparking self-sabotage or self-criticism, I encouraged them to celebrate the moment when they performed a clowning act poorly.

"Never mind if you were good or bad. Don't judge yourself. Just dive headfirst into the experience and tell yourself 'bravo' every time you feel stupid and vulnerable."

Many questioned if I was serious or if it was part of the clown act!

"Yep. Congratulate yourself every time you fail, because the more you do it, the more you will normalize the vulnerability, and the more comfortable you will become."

The message did not fall on deaf ears. A French trampolinist named Mathieu applied the concept to a T. He embraced as many vulnerable moments as he could, and after only a few months of artistic training, he converted from a timid acrobatic athlete to an outstanding circus artist with exceptional stage presence. The transformation was remarkable.

Baseball is a great example of working with failure. Did you know that baseball scoreboards display the number of mistakes made by each team? As if making the mistake was not embarrassing enough, it must show on the board as well. Another example is that the best hitters are unsuccessful 7 times out of 10 attempts at the plate. That's right; a hitter with a .300 batting average is considered an all-star player. Baseball players pocket millions of dollars from failing more than succeeding. In 2019, Los Angeles Angels star player Mike Trout earned $33 million, which is a payout of approximately $70,000 per at-bat. That year he struck out a whopping 120 times. But his failures did not stop him; by accepting the Oops moments, Trout stayed focused and was able to crank the ball out of the park 45 times.

Whether it is playing baseball, becoming a circus artist or putting together a winning team, you must create an environment

If you're
not failing,
**what you're
doing is not
hard enough.**

where failure is accepted and encouraged. You should even celebrate the mistakes. I am not suggesting throwing a party for every bad performance, but bringing in some silliness can help athletes relax and learn to play with mistakes.

André put forth the Oops concept in a brilliant, yet unusual way with the national women's baseball team. One of his childhood heroes was Patof, a clown he idolized on TV. Patof would get in trouble from making blunders and getting caught in slip-ups. But he would always find a way to bounce back.

After games, the whole team would share their nominees for the best Oops moment of the game, and the winner had to wear a T-shirt André had made with Patof's face printed on it. It was always a funny moment. The concept caught fire. Highlighting the Oops moments, and having a good chuckle about them, created a positive relationship with mistakes. The impact of failure was lowered thanks to Patof. The concept also influenced the team culture. Athletes took more risks and were not afraid of criticism.

From time to time, André would award the T-shirt to coaches so players understood that staff members made mistakes as well. This entertaining post-game debrief was not only about showcasing the Oops moment but also about providing an opportunity to come up with lessons learned for the whole team. It became a fabulous team chemistry booster as well.

Welcoming, accepting and celebrating failure must be part of your coaching philosophy. Acknowledge and recognize all efforts and attempts taken by athletes, even if they led to mistakes. That is how teams grow. You do not win games by playing safe. Success comes from going for it. To use a baseball analogy: you cannot steal second base by keeping your foot on first base.

Here is a series of questions to make you think about your relationship with failure:

- How do you react when your team loses? Are you overwhelmed with frustration? Do you accept the situation or reject it?
- How do you manage an athlete who plays poorly? Do you punish the athlete by benching them, or do you offer opportunities to help them bounce back and recover from a bad performance?
- How do you manage your own failures and mistakes? Do you keep them to yourself? Are you able to admit them to others?
- Could your team benefit from using a concept like André's Patof T-shirt? If not a T-shirt, maybe a funny-looking trophy or a medal?
- What kind of body language do you portray when your team is playing poorly? Does it convey acceptance?
- Are the athletes on your team comfortable making mistakes?
- When an athlete is clearly heading in the wrong direction, are you patient and do you let them learn by themselves? Or are you quick to redirect the athlete to the right path?

We challenge you to welcome, embrace, normalize and celebrate Oops moments. By doing so, many great lessons will emerge for you and your team.

CHAPTER 7: LEADER(OF THE)SHIP

We copy, imitate and replicate, all the time. Think of domestic pets. Is it not fascinating how, often times, a dog will share similar behavioural traits with their owner? The same goes for children. As they grow older, they often talk and behave like their parents. The apple does not fall far from the tree, as they say.

This resemblance phenomenon happens because we are social beings, so naturally our beliefs and behaviours are influenced by the people that surround us. In a sports context, the coach is often the person athletes spend the most time with. In addition, for some athletes, their coach is the individual they trust the most in their lives — even more than parents, teachers and friends. Like dogs and children, athletes might copy you by adopting your expressions and body language.

The way you speak and act can positively impact the team. Sure, there are other factors that help teams become successful, like using better communication, having a clear mission and coming up with a unique brand. But one of the most natural and authentic ways to create a winning team is for you, the coach, to simply lead by example.

Think of any sport dynasty and chances are, there was an out-standing leader who led the charge. Some examples:

- The NHL's Montreal Canadiens, who tore up the league during the 1970s, winning five Stanley Cups? The one and only Scotty Bowman.
- The NBA's Chicago Bulls, who captured six championship titles during the 1990s? The Zen master Phil Jackson.
- The MLB's New York Yankees, who dominated professional baseball during the latter part of the 1990s and the early 2000s? The legendary Joe Torre.

These three exceptional leaders were visionaries, unifiers and excellent tacticians. But most important, they were influencers. Their personalities were so charismatic that the players on these championship teams had no choice but to give their all, because their coach gave their all. Their imposing demeanour kept the players accountable.

As a leader, you steer the ship and everyone else follows your lead. If you steer the ship in the right direction, the team will flourish and reach its destination. If you steer it in the wrong direction, your team will struggle, and chances are you will get fired or be asked to step aside. In professional sports, coaches typically get the hook before athletes. What determines how long you will keep your job depends almost entirely on how well the team performs, which is ultimately a reflection of your own performance.

We truly believe that to get a team to perform exceptionally well, the coach must be the best performer on the team. You might think, "Athletes are the ones who perform, not me," but your performance is more meaningful to the team than you think. This chapter offers tips to help you stay on top of your game.

PERFORM LIKE AN ATHLETE

Athletes rely on a set of performance skills to compete at their best. They train, fine-tune and prepare for hours and hours, so they are ready to go when it is time to shine. How much do you prepare for games, matches or competitions? We are not talking about tactics and specific game plans to beat the competition. We are referring to your own performance. Are you ready to feel the pressure? Do you have the required skills to react constructively to unforeseen circumstances? Are you able to keep a positive attitude when your team is performing poorly?

Here are a few suggestions to help uplift your coaching game.

Self-talk and Affirmations

Several hundred thoughts run through your mind every time you manage a team during a game. What does your self-talk sound like in the heat of the moment? Pressure-cooker moments can crush you if you are not ready. Have a series of affirmations ready that you can repeat over and over when needed, such as:

- I will remain calm and collected when the pressure is on.
- I will find solutions to every challenging moment.
- I am well prepared to perform at my best.
- I will talk slowly, clearly and softly when athletes need advice.

The brain believes what it hears. The more you repeat your affirmations, the more you will remember and believe them. Athletes use them all the time, and coaches should as well.

Rituals and Warm-ups

Athletes never approach a competition without properly warming up. The same should be true for coaches. Do you have a pre-game routine? Do you follow a step-by-step process to get your head in the game? As a mental performance coach, my role is critical before, during and after competitions. I must be sharp and focused, all the time. When I travel to competitions, I make sure I am in the best mental, physical and emotional states. I am very disciplined about my preparation routine:

- I get restful sleep at night; at least eight hours.
- I eat healthy meals that give me optimal energy, and I pack my bag with plenty of snacks to help me maintain energy throughout the day.
- I work out for one hour — for example, I jog outside or lift weights in the gym — to release stress and sharpen my focus.
- I write important information in my notepad, such as key reminders about the athlete's upcoming performance.
- I visualize scenarios that could potentially happen, like staying calm while having a meaningful conversation with an athlete during a pressure moment. Mentally rehearsing situations boosts my confidence; I feel like I am ready to handle any situation that could arise.

By helping several coaches develop a pre-game routine, I have noticed many benefits, including:

- It offers a sense of familiarity, especially in a new environment.
- It forces you to stay busy by paying attention to useful information.

- It enhances feelings of control and confidence because you are optimally prepared.
- It diminishes overthinking, which in turn reduces unnecessary anxiety.

BE A LIFELONG LEARNER

As leader of your team, you are constantly wondering what can be done to help the team get better: *What needs to be polished? Which drills should we prioritize during the next practice? How can we play better as a unit?* You are always searching for ways to help the team reach its full potential.

But what about you? Are you asking questions about yourself? What are you doing to tap into your full potential? Are you getting better as a coach? Below are some great examples of how coaches can get better.

Educate Yourself, Every Day

Do not wait for others to tell you to learn; initiate the learning opportunities on your own based on your needs. Need to communicate better? Read the book *Made to Stick*. Need to deal better with vulnerability? Learn about Brené Brown's work. Need to give better presentations? Look up Garr Reynolds's books and seminars. With the internet, learning opportunities are endless. Personally, I make sure I read at least 20 minutes every night before going to bed. The books I choose always target a skill I want to improve. Nobody forces me to do this, I choose to do it. If reading is not your thing, then watch YouTube videos, listen to podcasts or attend seminars or conferences. Athletes train to get better every day, so you should also follow the same recipe.

Stay Updated

Why does your computer run updates periodically? Because the software would become outdated and competing companies would run away with the market, leaving your computer in the dust. Even though realities in sport do not change as quickly as technology does, you still must revise, stay up to date and modernize your approach. Let's take the three legendary coaches mentioned earlier as examples. In addition to the five championships won during the 1970s, Bowman won a sixth Stanley Cup in 1992 with the Pittsburgh Penguins and three more with the Detroit Red Wings in 1997, 1998 and 2002. There were 29 years between the first and last championship! Because hockey tactics and sports sciences were evolving, Bowman had to adapt and update his coaching style to remain successful over three decades.

Phil Jackson could not coach Kobe Bryant the same way he coached Michael Jordan: he had to adapt. For years, MLB teams scratched their heads, trying to figure out how to beat the powerful Yankees. Joe Torre was always a step ahead of the game. Stay updated or your team will become old news, fast.

Join a Mastermind Group

A mastermind group is a group of individuals, ideally five to seven, who share similar realities but preferably are working in different contexts. For example, my mastermind group is consists of six other mental performance coaches based throughout North America who work in various fields: NFL football, MLB baseball, the U.S. military, NCAA sports programs and the corporate sector. We connect on a virtual call, once every two months, to share our knowledge and expertise. I get to hear different perspectives, learn best practices, offer advice to peers and receive support from practitioners who understand my reality. Our conversations remain confidential, and because we all work in different sectors, there is no competition between us. It is a safe space to share freely and talk openly. Someone different leads every meeting, with novel and interesting topics, to keep the discussions fresh. At first it might be difficult to find a mastermind group within your network, but if you ask around, someone in your world might be able to hook you up; that is how I got involved in my group. If you have no luck finding a group, just create one. We cannot stress enough how beneficial peer-to-peer learning is, especially for a coach.

Have the Players Evaluate You

As coaches, we evaluate, judge and assess the players all the time. Why? Because it is our job to make them better and we do that by constantly assessing their performance. But who evaluates you? Your general manager, high performance director or team leader? Or maybe you never get feedback at all? The players you coach are well suited to assess the quality of your work — they are the recipients of your interventions. Plus, nobody spends more time with you than the athletes, with the possible exception of your assistant coaches. So, if you want the cold hard truth, establish an evaluation system that remains anonymous and allows your team to assess your leadership style, intervention methods and communication skills.

TAKE CARE OF YOURSELF

More than ever, successful coaches these days are fit, healthy, energized, calm, cool and collected. They take care of themselves. They do so by having S.E.N.S.E. in their lives: sleep, energy management, nutrition, stress management and exercise.

If you're coaching a high-performing team, **be a high-performing coach.**

Sleep

Block the number of sleeping hours you need in your schedule and organize all of your other activities around that. If you do the opposite, you will end up sleeping whatever number of hours are left in your schedule — not a good plan. Make sleep a priority. Create a sleeping routine. Sleep around the clock once in a while. Nap every day, if you can, for 15 to 25 minutes. When you are rested, everything else in your life is smooth sailing.

Energy Management

Do not wait until you are about to break to take a break. If you do, you will be chasing your energy all day. What do you look like when you are coaching? Sluggish or peppy? You must pace yourself or you will burn out. Take breaks, often. You mandate athletes to recover properly throughout the day, week and month. Well, walk your own talk.

Nutrition

Food and hydration are your fuel. Athletes work with sports nutritionists to improve their eating habits to maximize energy output and optimize recovery — have you ever thought about improving your nutritional habits? Your job is to make sound decisions, multiple times a day. You rely immensely on your brain power. Make sure you eat the proper carbohydrates, your brain's only fuel source, to have sustained energy, morning to evening. And drink water, loads of it. Did you know that a properly hydrated brain is a more focused brain? The better hydrated you are, the better decisions you will make.

Stress Management

Will you be stressed out at least once during the next year? Yes. Next month? Yes. Next week? Yes. Tomorrow? Probably. So, be ready to cope with it when it comes. The best coaches have go-to stress relief mechanisms that they rely on when the shit hits the fan. Mindful breathing is my go-to. To start my day, before a coaching session, on the bus to a competition or before going to bed, I take one or two minutes to breathe slowly, to flush my thoughts and be fresh for whatever is coming up. How do you cope with stress? My friend who runs a successful business reminds his employees, "If I'm not stressed out, you don't need to stress out." Your athletes are constantly watching you. As a coach, you must show a calm demeanour at all times.

Exercise

Nothing releases tension like exercising. Getting the blood flowing releases endorphins, the well-being hormone, which impacts our body language and mindset. Never underestimate a short, brisk walk. You need to change your thoughts during a competition? Step away from the group, walk for five minutes and come back with a fresh perspective.

Like using the oxygen mask in an airplane, you cannot help someone else in need if you do not help yourself first. Have more S.E.N.S.E. in your daily routine to better serve the athletes on your team.

They look up to you. Your job is to show them the way by leading by example. Be the best role model you can be. The way you perform will impact the team, in good and bad times, so take your role seriously and strive to be the best possible leader of your ship.

COMMUNICATION

PROVIDING APPROPRIATE FEEDBACK,
ADDRESSING WHAT MATTERS MOST AND
UNDERSTANDING THE TEAM'S NEEDS

CHAPTER 8: PYGMALION

Let's go back to 2012. For the first time in its history, the National Hockey League held its annual All-Star weekend in Ottawa, Canada's capital city. The league's best players were in town to show off their talent during a skills competition and then compete in a friendly game. Ice hockey is like a religion in Canada, so this event was a big deal. I may be a baseball coach, but hockey is my second love. The city was buzzing!

During that same weekend, I was taking a leisurely stroll with my two kids in the streets of Ottawa. As we approached the Château Laurier, the hotel where the hockey players were staying for the event, my son wanted to hang out in the hotel lobby for a few minutes, hoping to meet some of his favourite players. As we walked in, I heard "André! What are you doing here?" A few years earlier, I had done some consulting work for the NHL Players Association and one of their executives had recognized me in the hallway. He was kind enough to invite my kids and me to have lunch in the players' lounge. My kids had no idea who they were about to meet.

As we entered the dinner hall, we were surrounded by several star players who were accompanied by family and friends. The setup was well thought out. There was a section to play video games, a lounging area with sofas, and a gigantic buffet to please large appetites.

A little intimidated, we sat down at the first free table we came upon. My son was quite impressed to see some of his favourite players in real life. Given the glorious opportunity, he made sure to take pictures with superstars Carey Price and John Tavares. We were all in awe, but what was most striking was seeing Zdeno Chára. At six-foot-nine, this giant stuck out like a sore thumb. In hockey jargon, he was a real beast. A year earlier, Chára had made headlines with a vicious bodycheck on Max Pacioretty, the Montreal Canadiens' top forward at the time. The hit had sidelined Pacioretty for several weeks. Chára had become the most hated player in the league for Canadiens fans, including myself and my son.

"He's a bad guy. I don't like him!" he said in my ear while eating pizza.

"Yeah, I know, he hurt one of ours. He looks mean!" I replied.

We were quick to judge Chára, without knowing the man at all.

Meanwhile, my daughter walked towards the buffet and got in line behind Chára. People were chuckling as they spotted my little four-foot girl standing between the tall defenceman and other big hockey players. Chára turned around, smiled, said hello and sparked a short conversation with my daughter. Surprised by his kindheartedness, I continued to watch him and realized that Chára was popular among the other NHL players. He noticed that I was eyeing him and came over to sit with us to eat and chat. I just could not get over how nice he was. I was wrong to judge him the way I had. Zdeno Chára was an absolute gentleman.

One of our downsides, as human beings, is that we are quick to judge people without really knowing them. We like to criticize at first glance and label people without considering their personality and doing any background checks.

Don't judge an athlete by their cover.

We judge news reporters, social media influencers, actors, teachers, co-workers and neighbours all the time, making comments like "I just can't stand so-and-so." Even though you have never met the person, your mind is still made up and there is no way someone will make you believe otherwise. In the case of Chára, I realized that what I had heard about him clearly altered the way I initially thought of him. But he was able to change my mind through his respectful and welcoming actions.

What if you have preconceived notions about one of the athletes on your team, and you begin to treat that athlete differently because of it? If you do not change your behaviour towards the athlete, you could actually alter the way the athlete thinks of themselves and affect the way they perform. This phenomenon is called the Pygmalion effect.

The origin of this principle goes way back. In Greek mythology, Pygmalion was an ancient Greek sculptor who fell madly in love with one of his sculptures. Over and over again, he imagined it as a real woman, so much so that at some point he altered reality and she became the very thing he imagined her to be. Similarly, given the Pygmalion effect, if we perceive a person a certain way, our behaviours towards them can be influenced by that belief and can cause their actions to change.

Over the years, different interpretations of the Pygmalion effect have evolved. We would like to take a closer look at one in particular: how unconscious prejudices can impact coaches' interactions with and their behaviours towards athletes.

Coaches come up with unintentional expectations of athletes all the time. These expectations can stem from various factors, such as:

- The athlete's country, city or neighbourhood (e.g., "He has Russian roots, he must be a hard worker.")

- Personality traits, such as extraversion, neuroticism or openness (e.g., "This athlete is shy. She will never become a team captain.")
- Past performances that demonstrated success, talent or abilities (e.g., "She racked up many points last year. She will become a superstar.")
- Physical attributes, like being big, strong or tall (e.g., "He must be tough with a frame like that.")

Coaches then subconsciously determine how they will behave, according to these expectations. A coach may demand bigger efforts, offer more valuable advice and be more attentive towards an athlete for whom they have higher hopes. But beware that the same phenomenon applies for the opposite scenario. If the expectations are low, a coach may unintentionally be more distant, assume subpar performances and offer limited feedback.

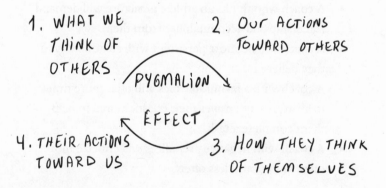

This devious cycle can be a trap, good or bad, because the athlete will then subconsciously determine their own beliefs based on their coach's behaviours. This could manifest as either:

- "The coach talks to me regularly/he seems to like me/he believes in my abilities . . . so I will work harder in practice." or
- "I never hear from my coach/I must not live up to her standards/I'm not important to the team . . . she won't notice if I slack off."

Fundamentally, everything starts with the coaches' biases, prejudices and preconceptions.

To help identify the victims, here are some typical behaviours of coaches who fall into the Pygmalion trap:

- A coach who perceives an athlete as weak will naturally avoid them, smile less at them, offer fewer learning opportunities and provide minimal support.
- A coach who does not trust an athlete will keep conversations shallow and short, and not share confidential information with them.
- A coach who thinks an athlete is mature will demand leadership and accountability from them.
- A coach will be more persistent with an athlete who they believe in.
- A coach with a favourable bias will offer more time to an athlete to answer their questions and to help them complete a task.
- A coach with negative prejudices will criticize more often and reward less often.

Considering some of these behaviours, it becomes next to impossible for every athlete on a team to reach their full potential. In most team sports, the sum of individual performances determines if a team will win or lose, so coaches must pay close attention to this trap, or some athletes will compromise the team's success.

The tricky part about the Pygmalion effect is that it stems from unintentional expectations. So, to counteract this phenomenon, you must have intentional and deliberate strategies that you apply consciously when coaching.

When you say, "My door is always open," but only a select few show up, it is a sign that you — either consciously or unconsciously — have shown favouritism. It is likely the athletes you believe in are the ones who are knocking at the door, but it's the ones who *aren't* showing up who might need you the most. So instead of asking athletes to come see you, you must go to them. Come up with tactics such as additional meetings, mandatory daily check-ins or extra time spent in other areas like the gym, therapy room or cafeteria to be around athletes more.

With the national baseball team, I came up with a concept called "breakfast with the coaches." During training camps and tournaments, four different athletes would share a meal with the coaching staff each day. It allowed me and the other coaches to spend at least 30 quality minutes with different players, every day. The goal was to speak about everything and nothing. It is fascinating how much we learned about them. Every single day we did this, some of my biases and assumptions were overturned. These breakfasts were perspective shifters.

Here is another great example. We know an experienced professional hockey coach who keeps a checklist with the names of every player on the team. He prints this list every day and places a checkmark next to each player's name every time he connects with them. It is his way of making sure he speaks to everyone on the team each day. The list not only indicates if he has been spending too much time with the same athletes — often this is illustrated by the number of checkmarks — but also shows which athletes were avoided or forgotten during the day. The list can inform him and allow him to diversify his encounters. He once said, "It's remarkable how much you can learn from the less popular athletes. They offer much more to your team than you think."

The Pygmalion effect happens subconsciously, but don't let it go undetected. We did our job in warning you. Now, it is your job to stay away from it.

CHAPTER 9: YOUR COACH

Golf is an interesting sport. It seems so easy when you watch it on TV, but once you start playing the game, you realize that it is much harder to master than expected.

Every spring, golf enthusiasts across Canada flock to the practice facilities in preparation for the upcoming summer season. For most golfers, the goal is always the same: to play much better than the year before. This year will be *the* year. Yet, with so much time spent hitting balls at the driving range, why don't most players improve? Can a golfer get better results from only hitting buckets of golf balls, over and over again?

Many coaches still preach the motto "Practice makes perfect." But what does this mean, exactly? Let's assume that, hypothetically, ongoing learning is part of your team's core values. As the leader of the team, this means that your main goal is to create a learning environment that will spark lessons learned for athletes and staff. Otherwise, no significant growth will happen. Having the team partake in robust training sessions will help; however, it is only from receiving meaningful feedback that athletes will realistically reach their goals. This essential communication skill deserves a closer look.

Let's start by dissecting the word "feedback." Essentially, feedback is when an individual receives information (feed) based on a performance that was executed in time (back). This sparks self-examination that may or may not improve performance, depending on the quality of information provided.

Athletes often evaluate their own performances through self-reflection. This form of feedback is valuable, but it may be skewed; since it comes from the athlete themselves, it is biased and may not be a realistic portrayal of the positives or negatives of their performance. There are certain important performance-related elements that an athlete can't become aware of without an external eye. It is only with an external source, like a coach offering some remarks or analyzing video clearly showing some technical flaws, that feedback can become complete and thorough.

From a neurological perspective, quality feedback can help myelin production. Made up of protein and fatty substances, myelin acts as a protection membrane for neurons (imagine the plastic that encases electrical wires) to ensure that electrical impulses are transmitted from neuron to neuron. The stronger the myelin, the stronger the impulse. The stronger the impulse, the quicker and stronger the physical movements become. To simplify the explanation, here is how quality feedback leads to better performance.

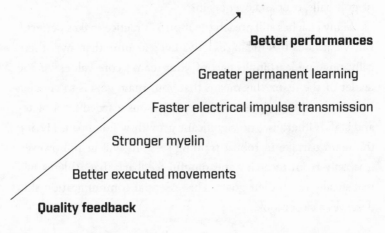

Better performances

Greater permanent learning

Faster electrical impulse transmission

Stronger myelin

Better executed movements

Quality feedback

Simple, isn't it?

Now, let's get back to golf. Practising alone can lead to some minimal improvement, but realistically, significant progress will only happen if you are getting recurrent, quality external feedback. Then, who knows, it may well be *the* year.

Frequent quality feedback is the secret weapon of most successful teams. When JF was working with Scott Moir and Tessa Virtue, he realized they knew all about the value of quality feedback. In preparation for the 2018 Olympic Games, these superstar figure skaters chose to surround themselves with 14 coaches, each specializing in different aspects of their performance. During a typical practice, Tessa and Scott would listen to feedback from their skating coaches every two minutes or so. They were constantly aware of what needed to be improved in their performance. No wonder they are three-time Olympic gold medallists.

We will explore some best practices around providing feedback in the following chapters, but for this chapter, I will focus on the value of you receiving feedback, as the coach.

When I coach, I constantly question how I can improve the feedback I provide to athletes, and so I love getting feedback to spark my own development as a leader. I purposely choose to go about things differently to avoid falling into patterns. My goal is to improve every year instead of being that coach with many years of experience who does the same thing every year.

I find myself reflecting several times a day, but like the golfer, I have acknowledged that only relying on myself is not enough. I need external feedback. As head coach of the women's national baseball team, I was responsible for the athletes' and team's development. I also supported the assistant coaches and other staff.

But who was my coach?

A few years ago, I asked an assistant coach on the team to become my coach; someone who would watch me interact and then give me feedback on how successful those interactions were. He was someone who I trusted and who I felt comfortable with.

Here are some real examples of feedback he gave me:

- "Melissa gave a great effort today. You hardly acknowledged it. Next time, give her more credit even though she didn't produce any points. She will certainly appreciate it."
- "Did you notice Patricia's reaction in the third inning? She didn't appreciate your comment about her play. Be careful with your expressive body language."
- "Your positive feedback after the heartbreaking loss was well received. Even though the team performed poorly, your feedback was constructive. This will help them bounce back. Great work."

These conversations were very beneficial. Many comments came as a surprise, giving me additional self-awareness and forcing me to reconsider some of my coaching habits. The constant feedback helped to improve my coaching skills. Most importantly, I became a better coach, and a better coach translates to a better team. Sometimes comments were hard to take, but I was willing to sacrifice my ego for the betterment of the team.

Thankfully, a coach for coaches is becoming more common, especially in the sports world. This individual can play an important role in an organization by supporting the professional development for the coaching staff. If your organization does not have a budget for this type of specialist, you can choose someone in your group to play that role for minimal to no cost, like I did with our assistant coach.

If you are uncomfortable being coached by someone else, that is fine because there is another effective option: film yourself.

Is the
team getting
the **best
version
of you?**

Why do we capture athletes' performances on video? To highlight the good and the bad so athletes become aware of what they did well, and should keep doing, and what they did poorly and need to adjust, in order to avoid making the same mistakes. The same can be done for coaches.

Have you ever seen yourself coach? Filming yourself can reveal so much:

- Your physical mannerisms: are you in control or fidgety?
- Your choice of words: are they supportive or degrading?
- Your body language: is it engaged or passive?
- The way you approach the athletes: are you calm or direct?
- Your tone of voice: do you talk or yell?
- Your posture when standing still: is it straight or slouched?

While doing his PhD, JF conducted a research project that analyzed coaching behaviours. One of the research participants was an ice hockey coach. For two 90-minute training sessions, JF filmed the coach in action. The coach was also miked. They then sat together to watch the result. The coach was flabbergasted. He could not believe what he saw.

"Wow . . . I look so mean . . . I keep using the F-word . . . I rarely give positive feedback . . . I give the impression that I don't care . . . this is embarrassing . . . no wonder I'm having a hard time getting my message across."

JF hardly said a word; the visuals spoke for themselves. It was a reality check.

The best thing about video is that it does not lie — it offers the cold hard truth. From that moment on, the hockey coach's behaviours improved dramatically.

Here is some food for thought:

- Are you receiving feedback on a continual basis?
- Who could become your coach: An assistant coach? A mentor? An independent professional coach?
- Are you humble enough to be coached? If not, are you prepared to change?
- Are you willing to feel vulnerable for the sake of the team?
- What will you see when you film yourself? Will you be proud or ashamed?

CHAPTER 10: HOW ARE YOU?

What do we usually ask someone we have not seen in a while?

"Hello! How are you?"

To be polite and respectful — but also out of habit — most people will answer, "I'm good, thanks!" and then fire right back with, "How are you?"

Instinctively, the response is, "I'm good, thanks."

Most of the time, the conversation then turns to meaningless small talk like chatting about the weather or highlighting some news. But how much information do we really get from that interaction? Not much.

In a mentor-mentee relationship, both would benefit if the conversation would go a little deeper. To make this happen, we suggest you try an alternative way to initiate a conversation.

To better connect with the person, ask them to rate how they're feeling out of 100, with 1 indicating that their situation could not be any worse and 100 indicating that everything is perfect. At first, they might be thrown off by the question. But eventually they will come up with a number.

Let's say their mark is 75.

Then, to find out what the number means, ask them to expand on why they chose 75. Usually, the person will reflect for a moment before offering an explanation to justify the number. Typically, individuals with great self-awareness will stay neutral and realistic, while dramatizers like to exaggerate. Regardless of the person's level of self-awareness, their response will always provide a pulse of their current state. As a leader, you get to hear how the individual processes their life experiences, and as a result, you also get to assess their needs.

In elite sports settings, coaches are around the athletes on a regular basis — at practice, in the gym, at competitions, on the bus. From mingling and socializing, coaches end up knowing the athletes quite well, so assessing their needs can happen organically. But for most recreational and amateur athletes, they can go for days without seeing or speaking to their coaches. If coaches are not cognizant of what happened between their meetings, it may hinder the quality of their coaching. That is, unless they inquire about it.

As a mental performance practitioner, I coach more than 40 elite performers that travel the globe to partake in competitions. I do travel with athletes from time to time, especially for important events like Grand Slams, World Championships and Olympic Games. But the reality is, I cannot be everywhere at once, so consequently, most of my work is done remotely from my office in Montreal, Canada. To stay on top of things, I rely extensively on clients to fill me in. Having them rate how they are feeling out of 100 significantly influences the approach I will take during the coaching session.

Recently, Super Bowl champion Laurent Duvernay-Tardif walked into my office. We had not spoken in a few weeks. He told me he felt like 95 and spoke for 10 minutes about why.

"Things have been great . . . My training lately is going really well . . . I signed a new partnership contract with . . . My girlfriend and I picked our next vacation destination . . . I am excited about my upcoming season because . . ."

Over time, this easy-to-use assessment technique has become so valuable that I can't afford *not* to use it anymore.

Here are the reasons why you should use it too:

IT'S A GREAT CONVERSATION STARTER

Asking athletes to rate how they're feeling out of 100 is a simple yet powerful question that usually leads to you learning a ton of information and hearing a a detailed rundown of what happened in their life since you last interacted. It sets the tone for a conversation. You just never know where it is going to go — sometimes, the explanation is shared within a few minutes, but other times, this question can spark a one-hour conversation.

Regardless of how long the answer isto this question, the response ends up giving a clear picture of the situation so the coach can focus on what the athlete currently needs. Realistically, you will never get nearly the same amount of information from the commonly used, "How are you?"

IT'S PRACTICAL FOR SELF-EVALUATION

Athletes are used to getting judged by coaches, fans, referees and critics. Quite frankly, most of them enjoy getting evaluated, and this includes self-evaluation. When asked to pick a number, the athlete must self-reflect to gauge their level of performance. It really gets them thinking. The reflection process makes them take a position based on their past experiences.

"Well, that happened . . . and this also happened . . . that training was challenging but this session went really well . . . so, my mark is 85."

Plus, athletes work well with numbers. They deal with statistics all the time, such as the speed they ran, the height they jumped, the amount of weight they lifted or the number of hours they slept.

Every digit has a meaning. So, when they come up with a specific mark, there is always a good explanation to back it up. The number itself is not all that important — it is the explanation that coaches really care about.

IT'S CONVENIENT FOR MEASURING PROGRESSION

This self-assessment method can highlight if the athlete has progressed or regressed from one session to the next. For instance, when a soccer player's number is 90 in comparison to 65 the week before, there was an obvious progression made during the week. Probe the athlete to explain the 25-mark upgrade. A little extra self-awareness on how they improved is never a bad thing. Moments like these become great opportunities for growth. As a coach, feed the conversation by highlighting some small wins and conclude with strategies to keep it up.

On the flip side, athletes might say 25 after saying 85 in the previous session. Emotions such as sadness, frustration or disappointment can flare up. Moments like these can catch the coach off guard if they did not expect the considerable regression. As a leader, you may want to throw away what you had planned for that session and focus instead on being caring and empathetic to support the athlete in distress.

We also encourage coaches to keep track of numbers over time to help recognize trends at different moments during a year.

How are you . . .
really?

This can become valuable data to modulate training blocks and evaluate athlete development over time.

HELPS YOU UNDERSTAND THE ATHLETE'S SELF-PERCEPTION.

High achievers are typically very hard on themselves. Their tendency is to undervalue what they have accomplished, especially perfectionists. For instance, an athlete might say 60 when they probably deserved a higher mark, such as 80. By listening and observing carefully, you will notice clues (e.g., negative words, demoralized body language, lethargic tone of voice) that lead to a more accurate assessment of how they are feeling. Then you can help the athlete realize that they did not have to be so harsh on themselves. You can also highlight that they merited more credit.

Another common reaction from perfectionists is to allocate more meaning to what is missing (expanding on the 10 percent missing) instead of explaining the positives that justify a high mark (90 percent):

"I didn't achieve all of my goals last week . . . I missed one pass in training this morning . . . I ate some junk food over the weekend . . . I didn't accomplish a personal best during the last meet . . . and that's why I have 90 instead of 100."

They can go on and on and on about the missing 10 percent. When this happens, help them realize how much energy and focus they put on the negatives and how they completely ignored what they accomplished:

"Yes, you are right, there are some things to improve. Now tell me everything that justifies the 90 percent that you earned."

Redirecting them to the positives can become eye-opening, especially for nitpickers. They realize how negative they were being by dramatizing minimal flaws, basically making a big deal out of practically nothing.

Some athletes that become familiar with the assessment exercise take it very seriously. Snowboarder superstar Max Parrot is a great example. Occasionally, he will shout out his mark even before I have the chance to ask.

"Hey JF. My mark is 92 today. You want to know why? Let me tell you all about it!"

For some athletes, numbers like 89 and 92 would mean the same thing, but not for Max. His explanation would be different. His self-awareness is so developed that differentiating between small variations becomes an easy task. No wonder he dominates his sport as much as he does.

An alternative to this exercise is to use it with teams. For instance, each individual in a team will rate themselves out of 100. Then you add the numbers and divide the total by the number of athletes to get an average score that reveals the current pulse of the team. Of course, the individual scores also reveal who is thriving and who is struggling.

Another way to use this technique is to ask athletes and support staff to rate the team out of 100 to get a sense of what people think about the team's performances.

Parents can also use this assessment technique to ask their child how a game or practice was. It will lead to a more detailed conversation instead of just getting a short-ended answer, such as "good."

If you want to bring the exercise a little further, you can ask someone to give separate ratings for their personal and professional lives. It may provoke an interesting conversation about discrepancies and similarities in someone's life.

This assessment technique is important because, over the years, we noticed that coaches will often plan training sessions based entirely on where they left off from the previous session. This means workouts, drills and discussions are decided based on where the athlete was instead of where the athlete is in their current developmental process. To ensure proper teaching and guidance, you must dig a little deeper when inquiring about the athlete's current state. Nobody knows their needs as much as they do.

So, next time you are about to ask how an athlete is doing, keep in mind that there is a better way of assessing someone's current situation that can really go a long way. Before heading to the next chapter, what is your rating out of 100, right now? And, why?

CHAPTER 11: P.R.P.

Here is a situation that happens regularly during practices.

The team is working well, battling hard during drills to get ready for the upcoming competition. So far, you like what you are seeing. You and the assistant coaches are satisfied with the team's effort. The practice is running smoothly. Suddenly, while the team is polishing a specific team strategy, you notice something that starts bugging you. You let it slide once, but then it happens again, and again. You immediately blow the whistle to halt the drill. The athletes know very well that, by stopping the play, it means something is not to your liking. Typical reactions from athletes are the following:

"What'd we do wrong? What's the coach going to tell us? Did I do something I wasn't supposed to do? Was it my fault? I hope it's not me!"

At this particular moment, most athletes are looking down to avoid eye contact with you.

What is about to come out of your mouth to address the situation will be one of three options. The feedback will be targeted towards (1) the **P**erson (or the team), (2) the **R**esult or (3) the **P**rocess.

PERSON (OR THE TEAM)

This type of feedback is addressed to the individual(s), referring to personality traits or behaviours specifically associated with the person(s) concerned. Examples are:

- "You always miss."
- "You are dragging the team down."
- "Come on, wake up."
- "You are not focused."
- "You are not a good shooter."

Often coaches will provide this type of feedback when they are emotional. Comments can be impulsive and made without reflecting on the choice of words. Be very careful when directing your comments to a specific person, especially when the information is critical and hard to accept. Athletes can take your comments very personally and the effect can become detrimental to their self-esteem.

I still remember when my hockey coach called me out with harsh words in front of everyone in the dressing room, saying that my poor play was making the team lose. I felt so small and I just wanted to leave. Even though his remarks were only directed at me, it also affected the team negatively as some of my teammates were mad at the coach for showing such disrespectful behaviour. If you must share criticism that is specific to one individual, my recommendation would be to do it separately from the group, somewhere aside where you can still remain seen but the conversation remains private between you and the athlete (e.g., off to the sidelines, near the stands, next to the water fountain).

A useful tip to avoid personal attacks is by commenting on the person's actions, not the person. For example, instead of saying, "You suck today," mention that the effort is off today. The difference is subtle, but the negative effect is not as harsh.

RESULT

This type of feedback stems from the outcome of a performance, such as poor execution of a task:

- "Stop missing."
- "The passes are missing. Do it right, please!"
- "Your positioning is off."
- "The ball is not moving fast enough."

Commenting on a result is somewhat easy. You see something happening and then provide remarks based on your observations. It is fascinating how many coaches will make obvious comments, especially when their team plays poorly, as if the athletes did not notice the alarming situation themselves. Do you really need to remind your team of their struggles? Imagine if every time you made a bad coaching decision during a competition, people reminded you how stupid your choices were? Not necessary, right? Well, the same goes for the athletes.

As a mental performance coach, I analyze how coaches communicate all the time. I noticed that approximately 80 percent of feedback provided is based on the person or the result. Why? Probably because it is easier to comment on a person's behaviour or the outcome of a performance because they are obvious to point out. But the third type of feedback demands a little more reflection.

PROCESS

This type of feedback alludes to steps, procedures and methods related to a performance outcome:

- "You are missing the net because you're not looking where you're shooting."
- "You were trying to go too fast and that's why your passes are off the mark."
- "The passes are getting intercepted because the execution is too slow and telegraphed."
- "You are flat and sluggish because of your lack of effort."

While the first two types of feedback scratch the surface, process-oriented feedback provides a deeper explanation for athletes to understand the outcome of their behaviours. Because the content is more profound and detailed, it requires more thinking before talking. Of course, this is the most difficult option to stick to, especially in the heat of the moment. But in the end, I encourage you to choose process-related feedback as much as possible because it is the one that will spark team growth the most. (See chapter 15, "Lego," for more details.)

While the main goal of this chapter is to help you reflect on the type of feedback you provide to athletes, there is another important nugget to take away. From studying and analyzing communication within teams, we noticed that most coaches have a misconception that feedback is mostly provided by an authority figure to a learner. For example, the coach to the athlete. However, we have noticed that more than 50 percent of feedback given or received within a team setting does *not* originate from coaches — it is shared between the athletes themselves.

Have you ever wondered how many comments, tips, suggestions, ideas and remarks are shared from one athlete to another? As coaches, we tend to forget that athletes talk to each other all the time during practices, on bus rides, through texting and from hanging out together outside of the sports setting. Coaches not

Do your athletes a favour — focus more on **process.**

only need to become champion communicators by choosing the correct type of feedback to give, but they must also educate athletes on how to provide effective feedback to each other.

Athletes can have a significant impact on each other, so we recommend you take some time to expose them to this idea. They will become better equipped as feedback givers, which in the end will impact team effectiveness. For example, during a stoppage of play during a game, athletes must deal with several warring emotions, given the pressure of the moment. Knowing what to say, and how to say it, can help a teammate bounce back from failure.

You may have noticed that negative comments were used earlier to explain the three different types of feedback. The reason we chose this approach was because most coaches will stop a drill during practice only when something wrong is happening, like a poorly executed play.

Have you ever done the opposite? Have you ever whistled a play down to grab the players' attention and congratulate a great play?

Imagine this scenario:

You blow the whistle. Players stop, wondering what will be said.

"Hey everyone, listen up, I just wanted to tell you how amazing that play was! Wow! It was incredibly beautiful to watch. You clearly understood what we want you to execute during the play. Now, carry on."

Smiles will automatically appear on athletes' faces. Acknowledging great plays has so many benefits:

- It creates a positive atmosphere by boosting levels of satisfaction.
- It highlights technical and tactical elements that the team is trying to improve.
- It changes the meaning of interrupting a drill; not only because something bad happened.

- It brings additional fun and pleasure to practices, which can foster more resiliency in athletes' behaviours.

Give it a try. We guarantee that your athletes will appreciate the gesture.

CHAPTER 12: DEBRIEF

The game has ended, and it is now time for the coach to talk about the team's performance. This review usually happens along these lines: post-game, the coach gathers the athletes together in an area off to the side, away from parents, friends, media and any fans still hanging around. Looking at the athletes, it is easy to guess the team's result based on body language. Smiles and looks of excitement generally mean a win and a good performance. Athletes looking down or appearing sad or sluggish usually suggests a poor outcome or effort.

As the coach, you want the post-game debrief to be as productive and beneficial to the team as possible. To help you achieve this, we offer the following recommendations:

BE PREPARED

How are you planning to lead this session? What is your objective? What are the key points you want to emphasize? Who will be talking? Are you calling on the assistant coaches to share input? How long will the debrief be?

It is worth noting that the athlete's attention span is about eight seconds. We are not saying you have to pack everything into eight seconds, but if your message drags on, there is a good chance your team will not retain your key messages.

In order to maximize your debrief, keep a notepad with you and make notes during the competition. This strategy will ensure you do not miss key points during your post-game talk, and allow you to remain efficient with time and not forget anything if the discussion goes in an unexpected direction. If you wish to mention anything specific from the performance, you will have your notes as a reference.

AVOID DISTRACTIONS

If you can, be sure to talk with the players in an area with as few distractions as possible. These could include parents and friends or teams nearby preparing to take the same field for their game. Weather will also play a role in deciding where to meet. If you are outside, remember to consider the sun — it is better for one coach to have to shield their eyes than 15 players needing to do so. Making that sacrifice will avoid leaving the door open for players to use the sun as an excuse for not paying attention to you.

While visual distractions must be avoided, a coach being heard is of equal importance. This is even more critical if your voice is one that does not project very well. It would be wise to find a spot that is quiet, where background noise will not take attention away from your message.

Some coaches will conduct their wrap-up chat while the athletes are recharging during a stretch or cool-down session. While this idea might save some time, you don't get the athletes' full attention.

Time is also very important. Even if you plan to keep your debrief short, be careful not to be pressed by time to end early.

Take the time that is needed to ensure a quality debrief or you might leave out important messages and takeaways.

CHOOSE YOUR PREFERRED FORMATION

The way in which the team is positioned will affect how your message is received. As a general principle, try not to have anyone behind you. Make sure you can have eye contact with each of the team members to make the best possible connection. You should choose a formation that allows the athletes to see each other as well. Should any member wish to speak, they should be seen by everyone. Also consider the desired proximity of the group. A semi-circle helps to meet all these criteria.

Over time, we have observed and have used three different communication methods for conducting a performance debrief. All three can be effective and should be employed depending on the game context and maturity level of your team. Let's explore them in detail.

The One-Way Street

This solo talk goes in only one direction. The coach speaks, the players listen. There is no conversation, and no questions are asked. Usually, the coach goes over positive points and things that went well. The coach also covers the negative points or what the athlete or team will need to work on at the next practice in order to improve.

This approach can be useful when you want to send a clear message to your group or assert your authority, as can be necessary when the team is in the birth or adolescent stage in its cycle of development (see chapter 3, "Team Cycles," for more details). The team might be young and immature; or perhaps you have only been a coach for a short while; or maybe there is little connection between members of the team. While the one-way street method can prove effective to a certain extent, it will not necessarily spark a change in behaviour or help athletes perform with more motivation.

The Two-Way Street

In this formation we move from monologue to dialogue. Here, the coach acts as facilitator and guides the athletes in a reflection of the team's performance. Athletes are steered in a manner that encourages them to identify the answers to the coach's questions. Such a method allows for better interaction between the coach and players. Instead of the coach simply rhyming off the highs and lows of the game to the athletes, asking them open-ended questions about the outing can spur some helpful insights and observations. Here are some examples of questions that can elicit good reflection:

- "In your opinion, what worked well today?"
- "What should our point(s) of focus be over the next few days to correct mistakes or bridge some gaps?"
- "What are the technical elements that we practised this week that we executed well during this competition?"
- "What did you think of our team communication during the game?"
- "Is there a teammate who played particularly well or stood out to you today?"
- "How did you react after the referee's bad call in the second period?"
- "What can we do to be more prepared for our next game?"
- "What do you think was the reason for our slow start today?"

This approach allows for collaboration and enables athletes to feel they are part of the learning process. It could make you feel uncomfortable, as you may think you are surrendering control in sharing the conversation. However, you may be surprised by the comments you receive and, with a mature group, you might even walk away thinking, *The team gave me plenty of good ideas and answers. Do they even need me?*

If you arrive at this thought process, it might be a sign the team has graduated from the adolescent stage (chapter 3, "Team Cycles") and is now entering the young adult stage. Your labour is paying off! You are now sensing the players are feeling more involved and are beginning to engage and commit much more. This principle is at the base of motivation, where a sense of talent and contribution can provide athletes with the spark they need. While the coach's solo speech serves little good in encouraging team chemistry, the two-way street approach can do a lot more in that regard.

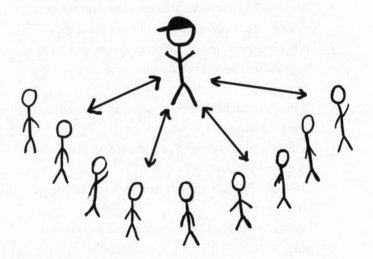

The Set-up and Shut-up

In this case, the coach puts everything together and then appoints a team player to lead the discussion. You now become a participant, able to answer questions if the designated leader calls on you.

This stage will surely take you out of your comfort zone and possibly cause you to become a little detached. You may also find it hard to resist the temptation to intervene if the discussion does not unfold in a manner you would prefer. You will likely find yourself biting your tongue at certain points, wanting to jump in and help the athlete acting as leader. Have some faith and let matters unfold as they will.

This stage marks a point where the team has achieved adult status (chapter 3, "Team Cycles"), which could prompt you to try this debrief technique on more than one occasion. Such a strategy will not only help develop leadership qualities for the person leading the conversation, but also improve their ability to provide constructive feedback. As coach, you can simply sit back and watch the show. This can be very gratifying, as you are able to observe the athletes blossom and problem solve collectively, learning and appreciating how answers are not always given by the coach but also gained through their own reflection.

Learning to navigate between these three techniques effectively will happen through trial and error. Recognizing that no

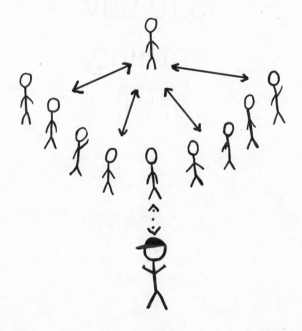

Sometimes,
the best
feedback
is to say
nothing
at all.

two situations are the same, you will need to learn from your own experiences. This will allow you to make more calculated decisions as the season progresses, and as you develop and mature as a coach.

A performance debrief is an important element in fostering team success. Be sure to include at least a quick summary at the end of each training session or competition, if not a full debrief. If you have access to a board — for example, a large whiteboard — use it to write down the key points and give your players a chance to take note of them or snap a picture with their cell phone camera.

Following a competition, feel free to share your notes or takeaways in online team group chats. Just remember to be aware that anything published will be available for public record.

Once your debrief has concluded, we recommend an exit ritual. This routine can come in many forms but will speak volumes about your group. Some coaches choose a particular team cheer, while others prefer simply giving high fives. Whatever you choose, the debrief exit custom is of great importance and should be communicated to the team.

When the debrief routine is done, you can now turn your attention to the real world. It is time to allow your brain to think about other matters beyond sports until the group reunites for the next practice or competition, or team event. This break is critical and facilitates a mental recharge often neglected or underestimated.

CHAPTER 13: WIN/LOSE

A coach plays a vital role in developing a team's ability to succeed. This role becomes even more important after a team performance. Whatever the outcome of a game or competition, athletes look to their coaches for a debrief that will help them reflect on their own contributions to the team's success. The previous chapter gave you tips for how to devise an effective debrief following a performance. This chapter will expand on how to best communicate with members of your team depending on the result of your game or competition.

Whether it's a huge victory or a crushing defeat, a coach's post-game speech should maximize impact. For example, while many lessons can be learned following a loss, we often forget that a win can also feature many teachable moments.

Let's explore some scenarios that coaches will encounter and identify some helpful strategies that can serve to improve a team's performance moving forward.

A TEAM PLAYS WELL AND WINS

Absolute perfection! The whole team is thrilled. Everything went according to plan and all members contributed to the team's success. As a coach, you couldn't be more pleased. Such outcomes, though, can be detrimental, as you can easily fall into the trap of developing an ego. It's at such times that athletes can often lose their focus and become complacent.

For a post-game celebration, keep in mind the importance of the game or the point in time during the season. If your win comes in the last game of the year, then sure, that warrants a big celebration. Go ahead and let the party begin, everyone deserves it. But if you still have games to play and a mission to accomplish, you might want to curb that enthusiasm for a while. Take a day off from practice and then get back to work. For example, after a big win over our archrival Americans, it was very hard for our Canadian baseball team not to celebrate. However, the responsibility of the head coach is to keep everything in proper perspective.

The temptation might be to not address anything related to why or how your team won, given that it would be so easy for the team to immediately fall into a party mindset. What a lost opportunity! Reviewing the ways and reasons you were victorious will reinforce the important points that will need to be repeated in subsequent games or competitions. Coaches can be very quick to question or analyze situations following a bad performance. But successful and disciplined teams put equal importance on doing a post-game analysis after a strong showing.

What behaviours, actions, special plays or strategies contributed to the win? Presenting this to the athletes can maintain proper focus on a team's upcoming matchup and overall objectives.

If a win snaps a losing streak, it is just as important to maintain the unity and connection among team members. Take advantage of this opportunity and use this win as a fresh beginning, a springboard to what lies ahead.

Maybe you can hold a bonding or team-building activity, like a team dinner, to keep everyone loose but still together. A year-end video reviewing the team highlights can also serve to remind everyone of the collective success earned during the season.

A TEAM PLAYS WELL BUT LOSES

Your team gives it their all. You're disappointed in the result, but at the same time, you are proud of the effort. It was a close game and your team is now feeling dejected. Such a defeat can lead to a loss of confidence. Athletes can easily wonder, "What good is there in a moral victory? What is the point of giving everything we've got if it doesn't bring us a win?"

Of all the possible outcomes of a game, this one stresses the importance of a coach's presence the most. You can't leave your team feeling down. The athletes need reassurance and a pick-me-up. They need to know you are proud of them and of how they never gave up. Take some time to talk with them, even if the sting of the loss may show. Be sure to also point out any positives that can be taken from the performance:

- Was the game plan executed perfectly?
- Did the team ever give up? Did they fight hard to stage a comeback?
- Did the players respond to adversity exactly how you asked them to?

With such a loss, it would be too easy but damaging to head home with only the final score in mind. No matter how disappointing the result, remember to mention to the athletes that with similar effort, positive results will surely follow. The tide will turn in their favour at some point. Never let an outcome become more meaningful than the effort.

A loss can also provide the perfect time to share stories of great teams that also experienced the agony of defeat. Pay attention to post-game sports articles in the news about teams or athletes that experienced similar outcomes. One day, you might be able to use them as an example, if your team is ever in the same situation. Think of it as developing a mental encyclopedia of anecdotes that you can reference to help give perspective to your future athletes or team. A loss calls for tempering the pain of disappointment, rather than getting over-dramatic or adding fuel to the fire.

Don't make excuses when athletes play well and lose. Never lay blame on a bad call by an official, an athlete's mistake, your opponent's behaviour, poor weather conditions or anything else. Always teach your team to take responsibility for their actions and the results. "We played well, but we lost. Let's move on."

You must never forget that competing at your best and laying it all on the line never guarantees success.

A TEAM PLAYS POORLY BUT WINS

You start seeing warning signs and hearing alarm bells. Despite the win, you detect a problem. The athletes are all happy and celebrating but you don't feel a great sense of accomplishment. There seems to be a missing piece to the overall puzzle.

An undeserved win can lead to a false sense of confidence, which could cause problems down the road. Remember to remind your team to stay within reality.

Use video clips to point out any underlying issues or concerns. If the schedule allows, this could serve as a perfect time to hold a practice as soon as you can to address any unhealthy habits you've observed. The quicker the team puts this episode behind them, the less likely the bad habits will continue.

A poor performance often follows a bad practice when the next game is against a weaker opponent. The more we perceive a situation as easy, the more we can take it lightly and the less we might prepare. This is how a seemingly easy win can quickly turn into a difficult one; even though you might get lucky and win, you might also experience a loss.

To avoid a negative result, I use the strategy of splitting a game into smaller units. For example, in baseball, I like to set a goal of taking one inning at a time. This places a focus on the short term instead of the long term, which is still unknown. With this approach, athletes can concentrate more on their performance and fundamentals needed in that moment.

Maybe you can apply this method in your sport, dividing a competition into quarters, halves or possessions? JF has implemented this strategy with a talented young hockey team. Winning games had become too easy for them. Complacency had begun to set in and the team had started to form some bad habits and suddenly they began to lose games. To get back on the right track, JF suggested to the coaching staff that they focus on winning each period, rather than the game. The young players really took to this objective. He remembers seeing the players standing on the bench towards the end of the first period, shouting, "Let's take this period, boys. Let's go!" The energy was electrifying. The team quickly rediscovered its form and ended up winning the championship a few months later.

As coaches, you have a big role to play in convincing your athletes or team that luck should never be relied on or celebrated.

A TEAM PLAYS POORLY AND LOSES

You can feel the pain and the loss of confidence. Despite this defeat, you have to keep the flame burning. Your challenge after such a game is to do whatever you can to draw some positives to share with your team. If you have trouble doing this, ask your team members for input. You might be surprised. It will also motivate them at practice to be prepared for the next game, or the next time they play this team.

The solution lies in a post-game analysis that reveals working on certain mistakes will ensure that your group is prepared the next time you face that same opponent. In a team sport where games follow a particular rhythm, it is normal to have a bad performance, or a "clunker," from time to time. The human body was not designed to maintain a high level of intensity for a long stretch. As long as such a bad showing doesn't become routine, it will be overcome.

After such losses, some athletes may be inclined to dismiss the situation, forget the game and move on. While a coach is wise to remind the team members the loss does not define them, I've had to occasionally manage situations where the team atmosphere was far too relaxed after a loss or poor performance. Having a short memory is often a good strategy but it is equally important to remember the frustration and embarrassment felt after a clunker. Taking time to reflect and concentrate on these emotions can lead to valuable lessons learned. This process might be challenging but could prompt some healthy and needed adjustments. A defeat can create learning opportunities that kick a team into a higher gear and push it back into the winner's circle.

A few years ago, I noticed an interesting practice taking place between teammates on the national baseball team. After an error on the field, the player who made the mistake would eventually return to the bench. They knew very well they were at fault. The tendency for the teammate would be to approach the player, tap them on the shoulder and offer some comforting words of encouragement. "Hey, don't worry about it. It's no big deal." The response from the player would be something like, "It *is* a big deal!

Leave me alone!" Often, the athlete wants nothing more than to be left alone. However, in sports, it is very hard to find a quiet spot to isolate yourself and process the moment.

During the 2015 Pan American Games in Toronto, I introduced a new strategy in hopes of correcting this problem. Before the start of each game, I always made sure I was the first one in the dugout and I would mark an "X" with athletic tape on one space on the dugout bench. Before our first game of the tournament, I explained to our players the significance of this spot.

"At any time during the game, if you feel the need to be alone or don't want to be bothered in any way — even if it's a pat on the back — you can go sit on the X. This will send everyone the message you just need a break. When you're ready to go again, just get up and rejoin the team."

Gradually, I noticed athletes using this option on occasion for short amounts of time. However, I recall one instance when a player stayed a full hour on the X! I myself have sat down on the X a few times, as well. Without me having to say a single word, the players knew automatically that I was not happy with the way things were going.

It is good to let athletes work through their mistakes. (See chapter 6, "Oops," for more details.) Keep calm. Your chat with them shouldn't be very long. In fact, it is very likely they already know how their mistake happened, along with its significance.

Following any potential performance scenario, regardless of whether the team wins or loses, your coaching presence is required. You can't avoid or escape these situations, letting the athletes fend for themselves. Get ahead of the problems and put your leadership in action.

Win or lose,
which
approach
will **you**
choose?

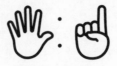

CHAPTER 14: 5:1

Have you ever come across a Mister, or Miss, Know-It-All? You know, the coach who has an opinion on everything. The coach who has answers to every problem. Because they see themselves as the expert, they need to prove it to everyone.

Is this you?

Obviously, not every coach acts like this. However, we have noticed that this type of behaviour is not unusual. It is especially common with:

- Inexperienced coaches who want to prove themselves
- Coaches who lack confidence in their skill set
- Coaches who are afraid to show vulnerability
- Perfectionist coaches who must have a solution to everything or they feel like a failure

These coaches share a common trait: they are very quick to offer advice. However, offering quick advice is not always the problem. The real problem is offering advice without considering important details that could have improved the information provided.

That is when our 5:1 technique comes in handy — ask five

questions (more or less) before offering one piece of advice. Let's give it a try.

Pretend you are a basketball coach. Thomas, who is an athlete on the team, shows up at your office, looking for advice.

"Coach, I have a situation and I need your help. Mark keeps making fun of me in front of the others. I'm not sure why he does it, but I don't like it. I don't know what to do!"

You fire back:

"Well, just tell Mark how you feel, I'm sure he will understand." As if it were that simple!

or

"Yeah, I know, Mark isn't the best teammate, don't worry about it, just ignore him." In other words, Thomas, there is no problem here, let it slide.

or

"Leave it to me, I'll take care of it!" Of course, you will, because you are the boss.

Some coaches will purposely keep a conversation short and provide quick advice for different reasons:

- Because it is their job to come up with answers
- Because they want to stay in control and avoid vulnerability
- Because they do not know what else to say
- Because that is what they said to someone in the past for a similar situation
- Because they do not have the time to deal with this
- Because that is how their coach managed these situations

Sometimes coming up with a quick response is the right thing to do. But in this case, Thomas is looking for support and guidance, and instead, you offered a command.

Let's deal with the same scenario, but this time, using our 5:1 approach:

"What is Mark saying to you exactly?" (Question #1)

"That I need to pick it up, that my poor play is affecting the team, that I don't deserve to be on the starting roster."

"I see. Has this been going on for a long time?" (Question #2)

"Yeah, for a few weeks now."

"And how do you feel when he makes fun of you?" (Question #3)

"I feel horrible! I feel like I'm dragging the team down. I feel pressured to be perfect all the time and avoid mistakes at all cost."

"I understand. Know that I don't think that you are dragging the team down, okay?" Thomas nods. "Have you noticed if he makes fun of other people as well?" (Question #4)

"Yes, he does. He also makes fun of the other rookies on the team: Steve, Peter and Cedric."

"Oh, really? Thanks for pointing that out. I appreciate you coming to me to share this information. So, Thomas, given that this has been going on for a while, you've certainly thought a lot about the situation. What do you want to do about this situation?" (Question #5)

"I'm really not sure, Coach. Mark is an important player on the team, and I look up to him. I don't want to create any problems. That's why I came to you. I really don't know. I need your help."

By probing deeper into the details of the situation, you suddenly have plenty of information to work with. In this case, you might continue by saying:

"Thomas, based on what you just shared, I see three things that can be done. One, I will keep an eye out to become more aware of Mark's behaviour towards his teammates, on and off the court. If need be, I will address the situation directly with him. Two, during our next team meeting, I will reiterate our team values of being respectful and encouraging others. These reminders are important for the whole team. Three, I suggest that you meet with the team's mental performance coach to help you manage Mark's behaviours a little better. The strategies will also be useful to navigate through other moments of adversity in the future."

"Coach, this is very helpful, I feel better already. Thank you for taking the time, I really appreciate it."

As a coach, collecting valuable data before offering advice is key. Although fictional, this example is easily transferable to any sport context. Here are a few nuggets to keep in mind when using the 5:1 technique:

ATHLETES KNOW MORE THAN WE THINK

Keep this in the back of your mind. Nobody understands the athletes' needs better than the athletes themselves. Today's athletes are well informed and have access to information in the palm of their hand. Do not be afraid to ask, probe and inquire. The better the questions, the better the answers. By probing their brains, they can help you find solutions to challenges, while also demonstrating great teamwork.

THROW THE QUESTION BACK AT THEM

This conversation technique is subtle but so powerful. I use this technique all the time as a mental performance coach. For example, just the other day, an elite track athlete asked me how to manage nerves two minutes before getting into the blocks. I threw the question right back at the athlete: "What do *you* think you should do during that moment?" Most of the time, an athlete comes up with great answers, like this runner, who said: "I should focus on breathing slowly, I should have more positive inner-chatter going on, I should bounce on my feet to get the jitters out."

Athletes
know more
than you
think.

I listen to the athlete's response to the question and then decide if the strategy is right based on the situation. But more importantly, this technique allows the athlete to come up with their own solutions, and when this happens, they are more likely to put these solutions into action because the answers came from them.

DO NOT BE AFRAID TO ASK TOO MANY QUESTIONS

See it this way: it is better to ask too many questions than not enough. At times, your questions will detect new information; at other times, they will simply confirm what you already knew. Either way, the questions will be valuable. When the questioning is not gathering any more valuable information, you have inquired enough and it is time to get into solution mode.

Before heading to the next chapter, let me ask you five questions:

1. Are you too quick to give advice to athletes?
2. Are there any other coaches on the team who give quick advice and could benefit from the 5:1 technique?
3. Can you think of anyone — mentor, former teacher or coach — who was phenomenal at using this technique, and could you learn from them?
4. Can you think of a recent situation when the 5:1 technique could have been useful?
5. Can you see yourself using the technique during an upcoming conversation today or tomorrow?

CHAPTER 15: LEGO

Human beings like to show off and demonstrate their strengths in one way or another. For years, talents have been displayed on stage. Skill sets are paraded in the streets. Special abilities are flaunted on television. Reality talent shows like *American Idol, So You Think You Can Dance* and *America's Got Talent* took over people's TV sets during the past two decades.

Nowadays, with the internet, showing off has never been easier, especially since the emergence of social media. Practically every post has to do with something good that happened or something exciting that is coming up, whether it be a personal best in the gym, an upcoming vacation getaway, a delicious meal or winning a medal in a competition.

It's almost nothing but the good, the best, the wonderful. Even though these posts do not represent our day-to-day reality, we still choose to flash the positives to look good.

Why do we not feel as inclined to share our vulnerable side with the world, like our worries, our weaknesses and our problems? For instance, think of a moment when you were in a rut and things were not going your way, and you shared what was really on your mind:

"I feel horrible today / I am distracted by my negativism / I hate my sport / I am unhealthy because of poor sleeping and eating habits."

Hard to imagine, right?

Even though we all experience these challenges, most of us choose to leave them aside. Instead, we pump our tires, hoping to receive as many likes and shares as possible to reel in new followers. We do it because we crave the attention.

But, why is that?

Social psychologists have plenty of theories to explain this phenomenon. Among them, the notion of "social worth" stands out. As human beings, we have a personality trait that is strengthened from being socially desired, accepted and approved. In other words, when we become more popular, our social status grows, and by default, we gain additional self-worth and feel better about ourselves. The effect is immediate. It is sad but it is true.

Why do we crave others' approval so much? Where does it come from? Many explanations exist. To shed some light on one hypothesis, let us take you back to childhood memories.

If you were raised in a middle-class household, chances are you played with Lego at some point in your life. Did you know that Lego has been around for more than 70 years? It was created in 1949, by a Danish carpenter who originally made the famous blocks out of wood. Not long after, they became the plastic blocks we know today. To this day, more than 400 billion Lego pieces have been produced.

Now, think back to when you were a young child: You are building a tower out of Lego in your bedroom. You are fully immersed in the experience, having the time of your life. At some point, you are done building and rush out of your bedroom with a big smile because you just can't wait to show off your new creation.

"Mommy! Daddy! Come see what I've done!"

And what do most parents say when they see their child's creation? "Wowwww! You are soooo good! That is unbelievable! Honey, would you look at that, our child is so talented!"

Many coaches do the same with athletes. The problem here is that these comments only acknowledge the result, not the process. The congratulations and the acclamations are only indicating "Bravo child, you're the best!"

When praised regularly, a child (or an athlete) becomes obsessed with the social approval. It is like a drug. They seek the attention, get their dopamine hit and then quickly wander off to do something else. In the end, there are no lessons learned from building the actual tower. But let's be clear — it is not the child's fault. The adults are the ones conditioning the desire of approval within the child's brain.

We are not saying that praising someone is catastrophic. What we are saying is that only praising someone is not good for human development. Our suggestion is to make them think, instead. Get them to reflect. Have the child talk about the process, so that they can understand how they were able to get to the final result.

Let us offer an example.

"Mommy, Daddy, look at what I've done!" (The child is seeking attention and approval.)

Instead of a quick "Wow," acknowledge the tower by saying, "Interesting," (or something along those lines) and then spark a conversation.

"How long did it take you to build the tower?" (Make the child think about the notion of time.)

"Oh, I've been working on this since breakfast this morning." (The child becomes aware of the time and effort invested.)

"Very well. Was this what you had in mind when you first started?" (Make the child think about the process.)

"Oh no! I changed my mind at least three times. At first, I wanted to build a house, then it became a small building and then

I realized that I had enough Lego to build a *huge* tower!" (The child acknowledges skills like creativity and adaptation.)

"That's great. Was it easy to build? Were there any difficult moments?" (The child will consider any challenging situations.)

"The tower fell three times, so I had to rebuild it. I had to put more blocks to hold it still." (The child acknowledges resiliency and solution-based thinking.)

"I can imagine. Great perseverance! Is the tower done or will you keep adding some pieces?" (Turn the conversation to a consideration of possible future steps.)

"Uh, I'm not sure. Hmm. Well, I could add another floor. Or maybe a big antenna. Oh, I know, maybe a helicopter pad!" (You have stimulated creative thinking and a plan for future improvements.)

"Those are great ideas! We are proud of you. Your tower is awesome." (Congratulate the child but only after making them reflect on the journey that led to the result.)

Then the child bolts back to their room to keep building.

In this Lego anecdote, the child receives much more than just a "Bravo." Because the parents valued growth and development, they posed deliberate questions to highlight the course of actions that led to the result. Without knowing, the child reflected back on the journey and realized important takeaways. Even at a young age, it is important to understand that bumps in the road are part of any endeavour and, as long as you put your mind to it, you can still achieve success. Through deeper conversations, rather than just superficial compliments and acclamations, children also realize that their parents actually care about what they are showing off. The extra attention devoted to the moment can build stronger relationships and develop profound chemistry.

On the flipside, if an individual is constantly applauded only for the product of their actions, it is risky, because their main motivation then becomes wanting to satisfy others. In the Lego

Hold
on to
your
WOWs.

example, if the child was only praised, they might build towers only to satisfy their parents and not because they truly want to.

Another negative effect to consider is developing a fear of disappointing others, especially if the child does not always get the big "Wow." Like we said earlier, the effect is like an addictive drug. A child might become hesitant to show off their skills if they are not certain of the response they will get. As you can imagine, this can lead to confidence issues or developing a fear of not being good enough.

Now let's bring this into the context of sports. Everything we just explained from a parent-child perspective is relatable to a coach-athlete relationship. For the same reasons, always praising athletes on their accomplishments is not beneficial. Great coaches know that asking strategic open-ended questions forces athletes to reflect deeply on the process that led to the victories.

I regularly use this technique with the athletes I work with, and I tell them, "Don't expect the big 'Wow' from your mental performance coach, you won't get it!" My motto is to always focus on the process, regardless of whether the performance was a good or bad one.

Long-time client Mikaël Kingsbury knows all about it. During the last two Olympic cycles, the freestyle skier won more than 80 percent of the World Cups he competed in. Standing on top of the podium has become so customary, it would be easy to say "Congrats" and then start prepping for the next World Cup. But I do not fall in that trap. After a victory, I pepper Kingsbury with questions:

- "How did your competition preparation go?"
- "Did you learn any lessons from your last-minute course inspection?"
- "How focused were you during your runs?"
- "Did you execute your pre-run routine properly?"

- "What explains your smooth turns in the middle section of the course?"

It is important to mention that I use the same approach during the odd subpar performance, so he can make adjustments for upcoming World Cups. I will congratulate the skier but only once Mikaël clearly understands the steps that led to the result, so that he can reproduce the useful behaviours during future competitions.

The same rules apply to a team setting. Pepper the team with questions. How were they able to win? What led to the success? Make them reflect back on the journey, the adventure and the procedures. Talking about it increases information retention, which can help the team repeat the good habits.

Having the players discuss the details among themselves can only improve team chemistry.

COLLABORATION

**FORMING ROBUST COHESION,
CONNECTING AUTHENTICALLY AND
SUPPORTING ONE ANOTHER**

CHAPTER 16: SOCIOGRAM

When I coach baseball, I do everything to encourage successful teamwork within my group, but sometimes it still doesn't stick. It makes me wonder, *What am I missing here?* After many years of experience, I realized the answer can often be found in the lack of connection between the players.

When managing a team, we are constantly faced with available information that could benefit us in tracking our team's dynamics. We should never dismiss this information, as it allows us to better recognize healthy or negative interactions among our athletes and help them develop stronger connections. Imagine a doctor making a diagnosis without checking all the test results to determine the patient's state of health. The task would be impossible and irresponsible. It is the same for a coach. Like the adage goes, "We know what we know, but we don't know what we don't know."

So how do we get this missing information? I have a suggestion to offer. But before I do, let me provide some context. Many years ago, the American psychiatrist Jacob Levy Moreno concluded from his studies that humans are connected by three possible relationships: sympathy, antipathy and indifference. In simpler terms:

- I get along well with this person,
- I don't get along well with this person or
- I am indifferent towards this person.

Moreno also perceived the following three fundamental principles concerning the dynamics formed in a group.

CONNECTIONS FORM QUICKLY

From the initial points of contact, group members begin forming bonds. These connections can be created through many means, such as a common interest or shared personality traits. This phenomenon always happens within sports teams, no matter the sport, size of group or level of competition.

THE MORE POPULAR ONES TEND TO GROUP TOGETHER

Often, the popular athletes are more vocal, demonstrate their leadership skills more outwardly and show their colours more comfortably. Those who gravitate to these athletes do so naturally, hence the expression, "Birds of a feather flock together." The same holds true for less popular athletes but, usually, it takes a bit more time for them to form connections.

THE DYNAMICS REMAIN STABLE

In most cases, the degree of connection does not really change over time. It can, however, gain or lose intensity. One should never take these bonds for granted and should always check to verify the status of the relationships.

Thanks to our many years of experience working with teams, we have made the same observations as Moreno. Just as good relationships will cement the bonds between teammates, tumultuous relationships can have the opposite effect. Evidently, like with any group environment, having complete harmony remains utopian. However, as group leader, it is essential to know as much as possible about your athletes and staff in order to best create and develop your team chemistry, even if some members may never get along.

Returning to Moreno, the psychiatrist became renowned for his work detailing the relationships, or lack thereof, between students in order to better understand the dynamics within a classroom. Moreno would present his findings using diagrams that featured many lines linking circles, resembling a spider web. From this, the "sociogram" was born.

Here is an example of how a sociogram can work.

When preparing for a world championship tournament, I must always submit a list to our hotel, indicating the names of players staying in each room. When playing in an important or high-stakes tournament, it is always a good idea to assign roommates by pairing together players who get along really well. There is nothing worse than matching a roommate who is super quiet with an athlete who loves conversation. As another example, if one athlete is an early riser, it would be wise to pair them with a roommate who has a similar morning routine. With this in mind, I create sociograms that help me come up with an ideal rooming list, and it also assists me in learning the pulse of my players' relationships and our team dynamics.

Here is my tactic. In advance and usually while on an airplane, I prepare small sheets of paper with two columns. The column on the left asks team members to list three people they would like to room with at the world championships. The column on the right asks each individual to list three people they wish not to share a room with at the tournament. Each athlete receives a

Connecting the dots can **reveal** lots.

sheet of paper and is told answers will be kept confidential. The paper looks something like this:

Column A	Column B
Three team members you would prefer to have as a roommate	Three team members you wish not to have as a roommate
1.	1.
2.	2.
3.	3.

The pieces of paper are passed around on the airplane and are returned to me within half an hour. At that point, I get to work, drawing out my sociogram for the left-hand column, which looks like this:

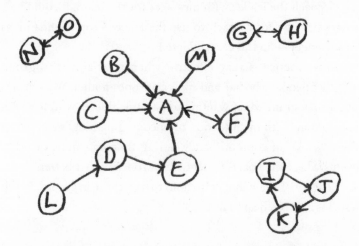

This example of a sociogram this example outlines the first choice of each athlete. As it is extremely difficult, if not impossible, to grant everyone's first choice, the idea behind asking for three selections is to know second and third preferences, thereby offering consolation for anyone not getting their first pick, while ensuring roommates are still paired well.

In the diagram above, you will notice athlete A appears to be the most popular. This often signals the player who will become, or already is, the team leader. You can also observe G and H, as well as N and O, chose one another, indicating a shared or mutual personality. Through the sample sociogram, you can also detect certain players not chosen by peers, while players I, J and K hold appreciation for their group dynamic.

While athlete A appears to be a leader-type player based on their receiving five votes, it is interesting to note the choice of athlete F as their roommate, possibly suggesting F has a powerful influence on A when it comes to making decisions. Since these two players chose each other, it's an indication that Player F can become a key individual for relaying messages to A that can be delivered to the entire group. While it could be a natural reflex to approach the leader with messages for the team, it could be a smart strategy for a coach to use the leader's top confidante as a messenger — in this case, athlete F.

This practice is very effective when your aim is to group together people who like and appreciate one another. You can also use a sociogram when wanting to pair up athletes with less of a connection, with the intention of encouraging bonding between them. This can come in handy during training camps or other events where the goal is to get to know one another better.

Be wary of these three situations that can arise in groups, which a sociogram can help to reveal:

THE LONER

This can set off alarm bells for a coach. You want to ensure this type of player still feels connected and supported within the entire group.

CLIQUES

Are there any groups that exclude others? Cliques are generally described as pockets of three or more persons within a larger group that typically only associate with one another. Do any cliques have a positive or negative impact on the rest of your team?

THE POPULAR CROWD

The popular ones are the people chosen several times on the sociogram. These individuals are usually appreciated and respected, enjoying good support from their peers. As a coach, you wonder if you can pluck a leader from this group who will then help motivate a collection of individuals to come together and form a cohesive team.

Returning to the information your athletes give you about their roommate choices, in the sociogram above, you can also use your findings in column B in order to make certain observations about athletes who might be less appreciated within your team environment.

Over the course of time, I have seen relationships evolve and adapt. A sociogram can be a goldmine of information that can help explain certain athlete behaviours.

Creating a sociogram can certainly be useful when arranging hotel rooming lists. But it can also be implemented in many other situations, including when:

- Assigning teammates for lines on a roster — three forwards in hockey, for example

- Creating groups for practice drills, either in a gym or on the field of play
- Developing roles and trust among coaching staff and personnel
- Assigning tasks to staff members working on a finance or budget project
- Choosing partners in peer-to-peer feedback assessments
- Making carpooling assignments

As a final note, always remember the sociogram is not an exact science. It carries its own limitations and should always be open to interpretation. Furthermore, when soliciting feedback from team members, confidentiality must always be respected.

No matter your approach, knowing your team better by connecting the dots will help you understand particular behaviours and make the right decisions for your group. As long as you remember this and trust your own experiences, something is bound to stick.

CHAPTER 17: GET PERSONAL

I was coaching a professional hockey player who wanted to polish his mental game. His goal was to earn additional playing time to contribute more offensively. Hard-working and determined, this athlete was ready to do whatever it took to make his team a Stanley Cup contender.

"I want to have more impact on this organization," he said.

"That's great!" I replied.

"Yeah, I want to play a bigger role. I'm ready to fill some bigger shoes."

"So, what's your plan? Have you shared this with your coach?"

"No. I haven't. Do you think I should?"

"Well, your coach is the decision maker. If you want to play a bigger role on the team, and get more ice time, don't you think your coach should be aware of your intentions?"

"Yeah, you're right. It's just that . . . he doesn't talk to the players."

"What do you mean 'he doesn't talk to the players'? When's the last time you two had a good chat?"

"A good chat? Ha! I don't remember! Maybe five months ago? Like I said, he doesn't really talk to us. He and I chat only once or twice a year."

"Once or twice a year! No wonder your relationship isn't great!"

You may be surprised to read this, but it happens more than you think.

There are still coaches today who remain impersonal and detached with athletes, especially in male-centred team sports. The authoritarian philosophies of "I'm the boss, you do as I say," and "It's is my way or the highway," still exist but to a lesser degree. Some coaches operate this way to avoid any personal attachment. It is a defence mechanism that creates a barrier for when disciplinary actions are necessary; after all, it is easier to punish an athlete if there are no hard feelings involved. In many cases, head coaches leave it to the assistant coaches to talk to the players.

Nowadays, most athletes do not want to play for coaches like that. Even back in the day, very few athletes liked playing for coaches who yelled at them, called them names or avoided their presence on purpose. But it was tolerated. It was the norm. Today, the younger generations prefer being coached by so-called player-coaches. These leaders talk to the athletes regularly. They care for the athletes. They inquire about the players' hobbies, families and other interests. They get personal.

Let us be clear on one thing: there are professional boundaries to respect. Getting personal does not mean crossing any line. Be smart about it. We are not insinuating that you must become best friends and overly intimate with athletes. We are saying it is important to be close to the athletes if you want them to be committed to the team.

The shift is happening. Interpersonal skills are a key requirement for coaches to get hired. Management teams are realizing that intimidating and impersonal styles are no longer welcome.

Have you ever had a coach who knew nothing about your family, your hobbies, your partners or your life goals? Were you inclined to go the extra mile for that coach? Probably not. Neither was I.

Think about the **person** **first**, the athlete second.

Going back to the hockey player example from earlier in this chapter, it's no wonder he was not invested in the coach's team system. He did not trust or respect the coach. He never felt like the coach genuinely cared about him.

Coaches often expect athletes to invest in training, which can mean being away from family and friends and putting aside other life projects for the benefit of the team/program/organization. But you cannot build mutual team chemistry from talking to an athlete once or twice a year, let alone expect the athlete to commit to the team.

Successful coaching is not only about winning championships and gold medals. It is about guiding human beings in the right direction, helping them flourish and making them better citizens for the future. Coaches should get to know their athletes. Making a personal connection will help you understand how to connect with athletes when preparing them for competition. Consider:

- Asking about their past
- Finding out where they grew up
- Inquiring about their hobbies and interests
- Learning the names of their parents, partner and friends
- Learning about ongoing life projects
- Finding out about their next holiday destination
- Inquiring about what preferences they have for food and music
- Asking about their life goals and their personal dreams

The last item on the list deserves special attention. When a coach shows interest in an athlete's dream goal, the athlete will go to war for that coach.

Lionel Woods — you might know the name if you are a volleyball fan. During his illustrious coaching career (which is 33 years and still counting) as the head coach of the University of Ottawa women's volleyball team, Lionel has made a point of creating a connection with his players.

After games, you will see Woods chatting with players' parents and friends. He checks in regularly to make sure athletes are getting good grades. He created volleyball camps so the players have summer jobs. He initiated an alumni program to create a family environment, connecting retired players with current ones. To spark more personal connections, he brings his wife and kids to almost every home game. Someone from my inner circle played five years for Woods, and 20 years later, she still talks about the positive impact he had on her life. Woods may not have won multiple national championships, but he has produced many successful teams. Most players he's coached have grown into successful human beings, on and off the court. Now, that is successful coaching.

We know a coach that used creative ways to get personal with the athletes. One of those ways was to invite herself for dinner. By coming into their homes, this coach got to witness the athletes' personal contexts, environments and realities. As you can imagine, players had different living situations: in an apartment with a roommate, at home with parents, in billet homes with host families or in university dorms. Attending 20 dinner dates was a big commitment but this coach saw it as an investment that was well worth it.

The coach had a philosophy that preached thinking about the person first, the athlete second. Those athletes' career achievements did not happen by chance. This coach got personal.

With younger athletes, some coaches will hold pizza parties in their backyards and invite all the parents to join in. This is a great opportunity to observe the athlete's interaction with their parents and to study how the athletes interact with each other in a more casual environment.

By getting personal, you improve the relationship between athlete and coach, and communication becomes stronger. Talking to athletes becomes easier. Saying the right things at the right time becomes natural. This skill is critical, especially in pressure moments.

Let us rewind back to 1992. A talented Canadian alpine skier is about to drop into the course for her final run during the Albertville Olympic Games. Only a few minutes are left before it is her time to shine. Suddenly, she feels an unusual amount of stress rushing through her veins. She starts freaking out. She turns to Carl, the team physiotherapist, desperately seeking help.

"I'm quite nervous all of a sudden . . . is this normal?"

In a controlled, calm and confident way, he smiles at her and says, "This is the most important moment of your sporting career, of course it's normal!"

They both laugh.

She falls back into her pre-race routine, refocused, and then down she goes. Moments later, Kerrin Lee-Gartner becomes an Olympic champion. Carl knew exactly what to say to make Kerrin feel better because he knew her very well.

The bottom line: the benefits of getting personal outweigh the drawbacks. If a player realizes that you will do anything to help them reach their dream goals in sports and in life, the player will do anything for you in exchange. Give and you shall receive.

Get personal.

CHAPTER 18: BUDDY SYSTEM

There is something comforting about receiving social support. It feels good to know that someone is looking out for you: to be supported, mentored and encouraged, especially when facing adversity.

Just think of academic tutors helping students achieve better marks at school. Or nutrition coaches offering sound advice to improve others' nutritional habits. These support programs exist because they work. They are about supporting one other, in good and bad times. Being able to rely on someone can lead to astonishing results.

So, how can coaches ensure that social support is happening within a sports team? Can it happen naturally?

It depends.

Given that human beings are biologically social beings, communal support can happen organically, especially when teammates get along. Athletes find a way to click, sometimes without understanding how it happened. However, when athletes within the same team do not share the same point of view, or when they have very different personalities, gelling is not always a piece of cake. In cases like these, putting a support system in place can help ignite chemistry.

Some years ago, I had to deal with some personality conflicts within the national baseball team. Two talented athletes frequently had heated arguments, putting the blame on each other to justify why the team was struggling.

"It's your fault because of this and this and that!" . . . "No way! It's your fault because of this and this and that!"

It was ugly.

The two athletes could not look past their own stubbornness, and as a result, they never took full responsibility for their respective poor play. Instead, they found excuses and put the blame on others. It created an awkward atmosphere within the team. Something had to be done, fast.

It was obvious that these players were never going to make up and get along on their own — they needed help. I had an idea. This baseball squad was about to discover a support system that would become a game changer.

The team was just coming off an unsuccessful tournament, and they needed to turn things around because the next World Cup event was just around the corner. Before their next practice, I asked the players to gather around.

"As you know, we haven't played well recently. We need to work better as a team. That must change. From now on, we will use a new team-based philosophy called 'the buddy system.'"

The ball players looked confused, wondering where I was going with this.

"The concept is simple. You'll be paired up with another player who will become your official buddy. Your job will be twofold. First, you must constantly show that you care, like making sure they are doing well and offering them continual support. Second, you will give them positive feedback all day long, like acknowledging a great effort, congratulating them for a small win and shouting out their name when they conquer challenges. Be creative, there are no limits."

Smiles started to shine on the athletes' faces. They were eager to start.

I gave my final instructions: "This system is about becoming a guardian angel for your buddy. You must do whatever it takes to fill up their emotional tank. At the end of each day, we will regroup as a team and share what our buddies have done for us."

The players were curious to find out who their buddy was. The duos were posted up on the wall in the dugout.

I took a chance by pairing up the two players who could not get along. You could hear some whispering "Ohhhhhs!" coming from the dugout. Within seconds, the atmosphere got tense. The players could not believe these two had to become buddies.

The greatest advantage of the buddy system is that it forces two individuals to talk to each other. They have no choice. At first it may be awkward, but after a while, the communication usually improves. Another great benefit is that, by talking more to each other, you get to understand your buddy a lot more by default. You learn to know each other better.

In newly formed teams, it is typical for athletes to judge and be highly critical of other athletes without knowing them very well. Too often, players do not give themselves the chance to learn about someone — their values, their goals, their interests. The buddy system can enable friendships to develop that otherwise would never have occurred.

And that is exactly what happened.

Thanks to the system, the two players who did not get along ended up putting their egos aside and focused instead on finding ways to appreciate one another. Surprisingly, it led to a long-lasting, respectful relationship. Getting them to make up was obviously beneficial for their own personal sake, but it was the team that benefitted the most from the evolution of their relationship. The two players were highly talented, and with less drama happening, their performances improved and helped the team play much better.

Supportive
buddies
=
Solid
teammates

When I first came up with the concept, I hoped some team-building benefits would come out of it, but I never expected what unfolded during that World Cup tournament. The athletes rose to the challenge by using the concept seriously. Their behaviours were creative and innovative. You could hear players shouting across the field, "Great job, buddy!" and "I'm there for you if ever you need me!" Players were going out of their way to high-five their buddy. Some did their buddy's laundry. Others brought healthy snacks and cold water bottles to practice. One of the players left personal letters underneath the hotel door, as an early-morning surprise, to make sure their buddy started the day on a positive note. The positive energy going on during practices and games was palpable.

The concept caught fire.

We ended up winning the bronze medal, which at the time was our best result ever. It was a great example that, when teammates transform into buddies, team chemistry flourishes.

There are several variations to the buddy system. Pick and choose some of these alternatives to make it right for your team environment:

CREATE SMALL TEAMS OF TWO TO FOUR ATHLETES

Building chemistry in a large group setting, like a football or ice hockey team, is not always easy. Timewise, it is not realistic for team-building activities to happen every weekend. But you can still form small team-building units, like duos, trios or quartets, to ensure that chemistry is happening in "micro teams" based on the total number of players involved. Choose the size of these micro teams based on your team setting.

MIX IT UP

Changing the buddies every few days can allow everybody to be a buddy with everyone else on the team. For example, for a basketball squad of 20 players, if the duos are different every couple of days, then every individual becomes an official buddy with every other individual on the team within a few weeks.

CROSS-POLLINATION

Pairing up athletes who play different positions will make the buddy system pollinate throughout the team. In a soccer club, for example, you can pair up a goalkeeper with a striker and a mid-fielder with a defender. Mixing up the coaches (and support staff) with players is also a great idea. In bigger performance organizations, like pro teams, you can crissc-ross departments, like matching employees from the marketing department with the human resources and finance departments.

SECRET BUDDY

This alternative is fun. Everyone on the team gets a secret buddy, and after a day or two, athletes try to guess who their buddies are.

CREATIVITY CHALLENGE

Having a buddy system competition can stimulate creative ways of supporting each other. At the end of each day, a trophy could be awarded to the athlete who came up with the most innovative gesture for their buddy.

The buddy system is like a fire starter. It ignites chemistry in smaller team units, but eventually, the effects spread throughout the team.

So, if you are looking to kickstart chemistry in your team, this concept is a team-building strategy to consider. Not only does it create a supportive working environment, but it is also fun and can produce results very quickly. What team doesn't want that, right?

Try it and you will see the benefits for yourself.

CHAPTER 19: INNER TEAMS

It is the beginning of a new semester at school. In one of your classes, you find out that a group assignment will account for a significant percentage of the final grade. The project requires six individuals to work as a team. After class, you approach other students to find out who wants to take this challenge on with you. Finally, you end up in a team with a few people you know and others who you are meeting for the first time.

Together, the team comes up with deadlines to ensure the project runs smoothly. The assignment starts well, but as weeks go on, one of the individuals in the team is not pulling their weight. When working alone or in a team of two, this individual tends to be a hard worker, but for this assignment, they are slacking off, doing the bare minimum and constantly missing deadlines. The other team members are getting frustrated. Everyone believes this student does not deserve the same grade as everyone else because of their lack of effort.

Chances are you have experienced a situation like this before. As a university professor, I regularly deal with students who share their frustration about slackers on their teams, especially when they know that person was such a hard worker previous to working in the larger group. This phenomenon is called the Ringelmann effect.

The French engineer Maximilien Ringelmann first identified the effect in the early 20th century. He noticed that there was a tendency for individuals to become progressively less efficient as the size of their group increased.

A tug-of-war competition highlights this effect. You know the game where two teams hold on to a long, interlaced hemp rope and then pull together until one team drags the other team over a central line? Well, if you pay close attention, you will notice loafers on each team.

The Ringelmann effect can stem from different causes:

- Athletes can slack off more when they notice other athletes are slacking off. (e.g., "Why should I bother if they aren't making the effort?")
- Some players will hold back when there is no individual recognition or personal rewards. This is particularly true for self-centred and egocentric athletes. (e.g., "What's in it for me?")
- Athletes can camouflage their laziness easier in a bigger group. (e.g., "The team will compensate for my diminished contribution.")
- A player's level of commitment can diminish from not understanding how to contribute properly to the team. (e.g., "My role is not clear.")
- A lack of coordination and collaboration on the playing field can lead to confusion and discouragement. (e.g., "I don't understand this play. I'll let the others figure it out.")

The last item on the list deserves a closer look.

Many all-star teams in modern sports history were unsuccessful because of a lack of chemistry. Take USA basketball for instance. Do you remember the "Dream Team" squad for the 2004 Olympic Games? This team was filled with NBA superstars like LeBron James, Allen Iverson and Tim Duncan. They were expected to win gold, hands down, but things did not pan out as expected. They struggled throughout the entire tournament, losing three games to Argentina, Puerto Rico and Lithuania, and walked away with a disappointing bronze medal. Elsewhere in the professional sports world, other powerhouse teams, like the New York Yankees and European soccer clubs, have been victims of the Ringelmann effect as well.

Players are often unaware of falling into this trap, and if they are, they will rarely admit to slacking off on purpose. Can you imagine if your teammate said, "I will take it easy tonight. Can you please play harder to compensate for my laziness?"

You will never have a winning team if several athletes think this way. It is your responsibility as the leader of the team to avoid this trap.

Legendary basketball coach Phil Jackson was brilliant at getting the most out of superstars Michael Jordan, Dennis Rodman and Scottie Pippen with the Chicago Bulls. He did the same with LA Lakers' icons Shaquille O'Neal and Kobe Bryant. Under Jackson's guidance, these talented teams left it all out on the court, night after night. The players gelled by playing specific roles and working towards a common goal.

There are several ways to dodge the Ringelmann effect; however, we will focus on one particular strategy that has proven to overturn the effect quite well. We call it having "inner teams." The strategy entails splitting the larger team into smaller units to increase individual productivity within a group. This strategy is especially useful when it is time to tackle important tasks and challenges, such as:

- determining team rules
- working on offensive and defensive strategies
- coming up with team goals
- fine-tuning pre-game preparation
- finding solutions to communication issues

Typically, smaller teams come to a consensus quicker than a large group. But we understand that dividing the bigger team into sub-groups can be tricky.

Who should be teamed together? What is the ideal number of athletes per group? Here are some tips to help you sort that out:

TEAM OF TWO

The good old pair. With only two individuals in the unit, each member is forced to participate and contribute. An athlete cannot hide in a duo. One cannot afford to be lazy because it would be shameful for the other member to have to pick up their slack.

A team of two is particularly handy for deep conversations involving important details, especially when emotions are involved. Duos are also practical for moral support and personal coaching (see chapter 18, "Buddy System," for more details). Pairs are also valuable for introverted personalities who are more comfortable sharing their opinion with only one other person and feel shy speaking in front of a larger group.

TEAM OF THREE

If you are not sure which option to choose for a situation, a team of three is a sure bet. Joining three minds is just enough to have an interesting mix of opinions and spark dynamic conversations. Like in the team of two, athletes cannot really hide and must participate. Adding a third individual in the mix is sometimes the missing link that a team of two needs.

Uneven numbers are practical. If a small conflict arises between two athletes, the third one can act as the mediator. The mediator role can change at any time when matters must get sorted out. Occasionally, two of three athletes can agree on one topic, and minutes later, completely disagree on another topic. When all three individuals agree on something, having a common vision can start to brew chemistry.

A team of three still offers intimacy while adding diversity, which is a great compromise between teams of two and four.

TEAM OF FOUR

Be wary of the potential outcomes when using this option. As an even number, the quad can break up into two duos. Divergence of opinions can create friction and set off an internal competition. Where is the mediator when you need one? If your goal is to spark some internal competition within a small unit, pick a team of four.

Groups of four can spawn two separate conversations at the same time. It can waste valuable time and take longer to come to a consensus. Keep in mind: the bigger the group, the easier it becomes to put someone aside. It also makes it easier for athletes who do not like being on the spot to shy away and hide.

If the team is going through a rough patch and athletes are in need of support, stick with smaller groups. We think that four-somes do not offer anything special, so it is better to stick with teams of three. But, if dividing your team in trios is impossible, a team of four can serve as an option.

TEAM OF FIVE

If you have a complex problem and you can afford to spend a considerable amount of time solving it, a team of five should be your choice. It may take some time for the five athletes to get organized and rolling, but once they do, great stuff will emerge.

This size is also big enough to witness the social and communal traits of athletes, which offers great insight into how they will behave in the bigger group. You might get to uncover some personalities that you had not yet discovered. In addition, it is common to see an athlete stick out as a natural leader who will guide the unit of five in the right direction.

In a team of five, there are 10 possible duo connections between athletes, which can create healthy interaction and collaboration. This option is highly beneficial if you want a variety of ideas and suggestions to emerge.

TEAM OF ONE

"One person is not a team," you might say. You are correct. However, we still want to mention that working alone on something can be powerful. In a group, there are few opportunities for personal reflection. Sometimes, not being distracted by someone in any group size is exactly what an athlete needs, especially when they have the skill set to fix the issue at hand. The same goes for coaches. Some matters are easier to solve with external advice, but if you feel confident about your opinion, stick to your belief.

Reflecting solo before sharing with others (in teams of two, three, four or five) is a great option. For example, an athlete reflects for five minutes to come up with solutions to fix the team's slump and then joins their teammates to discuss the slump. Time

You
can't hide
in a
smaller
team.

alone is an opportunity for deep introspection that can lead to great ideas.

One final note on the subject of working with others: The Ringelmann effect can bite leadership teams as well, especially in sports that require a large coaching staff. As with athletes, coaches can be lazy, slack off and let others compensate for their lack of commitment.

Be on the lookout.

CHAPTER 20: BE A CLOWN

Early in my career, I ran away with the circus. While I was doing my PhD at the University of Ottawa, I left the doctoral program to join Cirque du Soleil as their mental performance coach. Transitioning from an academic environment to a highly creative artistic setting was a life-changing experience, to say the least.

This is not just any circus. Cirque du Soleil showcases the cream of the crop in the entertainment industry — the best acrobats, jugglers, musicians, dancers, contortionists, fire spitters, singers, trapezists — from all over the world. Witnessing their performances is mesmerizing. If you have never experienced a Cirque du Soleil show before, put it on your bucket list.

For five years, I was privileged to coach performing artists representing more than 40 different nationalities. Working out of the international headquarters in Montreal was like travelling around the world, every day. I got to speak different languages, learn from different cultures and witness incredibly talented artists perfecting their craft.

Among the wide range of artists, the clowns were undoubtedly my favourites. Clowns are some of the most fascinating, interesting and intriguing human beings out there. For starters, let's talk about their profession. Their main role is to entertain people. At times, they make audiences laugh. At other times, they must divert an audience member's attention to fool them. To do this properly, they must strategically infiltrate people's personal bubbles to make them react to their shenanigans. That is not an easy task. It requires a combination of courage, poise and self-belief. They *must* be comfortable feeling vulnerable. Clowns cannot predict how someone will react, and their trickeries do not always pan out as expected. But the best clowns are unbelievably slick — adapting to unforeseen reactions is their forte. When they are on point, watching world-class clowns in action is experiencing a work of art.

Unlike most other performers who are on stage only once, clowns perform frequently throughout a circus show. Their performances are typically nestled between acrobatic acts, to connect one act to the next. The same way muscles hold a human skeleton together, clown acts hold the show together. They control the storyline. Diehard circus fans know that clowns are the heart and soul of the show. Clowns are connectors, uniters, but above all, they are master communicators.

Once, an experienced and talented clown from Europe rolled into Montreal for a few weeks to take part in a specialized training program before joining a touring show. Given his short stint at headquarters, I insisted on meeting with him, one-on-one, to pick his brain and learn more about how this clown went about his business.

On a beautiful Friday afternoon, I invited him to lunch to find out why he was one of the best clowns in the world. The lunch date ran a lot longer than expected.

"I'm so intrigued by your expertise," I told him. "Coming from the sports world, I know how elite athletes get ready for a match or a competition. Most of them follow step-by-step pre-performance warm-up rituals to get into the zone. But tell me, how does a clown warm up for a show? How do you get ready to perform?"

The clown fired back with unexpected answers:

"I use a 50-50 approach: 50 percent of my preparation is allocated to running my choreographies through my mind, making sure they are crisp and clear. Those choreographies end up being pretty much the same every show. They are very predictable.

"The other 50 percent is all about improvisation. My job is to goof around with human beings, and human beings are unpredictable. I need to be ready to respond quickly, to be witty. That's trainable. So, before the show, I take some time to imagine all kinds of scenarios that could potentially happen. When I do this, I hop on stage with full confidence. I feel ready to tackle whatever comes my way."

What the clown was sharing was music to my ears. I kept listening.

"If I relied entirely on my predetermined choreographies," he continued. "I'd be doing the show for myself, based on what I thought the audience wanted. No, no, no! Clowns perform for the crowd! We perform at our best when we are open to what the audience is giving us, and then simply adapt and adjust accordingly. And this is different for every show."

This is such a great lesson for sports coaches. We must keep in mind that, fundamentally, the act of coaching is for the athlete's betterment, not for the coach's sake. If a coach prepares a training session entirely based on what they think the athlete needs, they will most likely miss out on opportunities to adapt their interventions to better serve the athlete standing in front of them. Improvisation is beneficial for both clowns and coaches.

The clown had more to say:

"Tell me, JF, as a mental performance coach, when you communicate with your clients, do you listen to clients to respond or to understand?"

I was baffled by the question.

"Well, if you listen to respond, you're just waiting for your turn to talk. So, you're not really listening."

He was right.

"You know when you're talking with someone, and as you are speaking, the person is nodding excessively and is struggling to keep their words in their mouth? It's annoying, isn't it? In reality, they are not really listening to what you are saying. All that really matters is what they want to share once you are done speaking. They might hear what you are saying, but they are not actively listening. It is irritating and disrespectful."

I hate it when people do that. I immediately thought of a few individuals in my entourage that listen to respond, all the time.

"But, listening to understand is completely different. It's about paying attention to every tiny detail the person is sending your way. Their body language. Their tone of voice. Their choice of words. It all has a specific meaning. And when you pay attention to those details, you understand them so much better."

Clowns are amazing tacticians. Their actions rely so much on perfect timing. If they do something just a little too quickly, it does not give the audience enough time to react. If they wait too long, the opportunity can slip right through their fingers. So, timing is everything. To interact at just the right time, you must be fully connected and have a great understanding of what is going on. The same can be said for coaches. Sometimes, it is not so much *what* you say, but *when* you say it that makes all the difference.

Fundamentally, our brains are made to collect data, process it and then emit a response accordingly. Successful clowns know to trust their instincts. The best coaches do the same. They are not looking to force a response — it comes naturally. Their brains come up with a perfectly timed behaviour without much conscious reflection. Staying cool, calm and collected in the heat of the moment is key, so their brains can identify the perfect moment

The
**most precious
thing** you
can offer
is your
full attention.

to interact. Listening to understand provides the necessary information for ideal interactions.

When athletes are talking, take note of the following:

- Are they leaning in with excitement or holding back with apprehension about the upcoming task?
- Is their tone of voice filled with enthusiasm or concern?
- Are they using affirmative words or are they expressing a nebulous perspective to describe the current context?

Realistically, we can only adapt our coaching sessions by clearly understanding what the athletes are telling us, both physically and vocally.

This clown was not done. He had one more important lesson to share from his arsenal:

"I've learned over the course of my career that the most important thing we can offer someone is . . . our full attention! People like to feel felt. And when they do, they will embrace whatever you send their way. Presence is a powerful tool. People acknowledge presence. It never goes unnoticed, especially these days in our distraction-filled society."

How attentive are you with your athletes during training sessions? If you struggle to maintain your focus for extended periods of time, you are not alone. Let's face it: as a society, we have never been as distracted as we are now. It's concerning.

I remember witnessing a national-level coach looking at his smartphone more than excessively during a two-hour practice session during a World Cup event. It had to be more than 50 times. Being distracted will certainly make you lose your train of thought. How can you expect to coach properly when your attention is diverted every few minutes?

Is your smartphone with you when you're coaching? If so, do you really need it? Do you have a fear of missing out?

As a coach, what you are really missing out on are numerous opportunities to collect valuable data. An essential part of coaching is the magic that happens in the moment. Modifications and adjustments are made from connecting the dots as the training goes on.

We suggest putting your phone away when you are coaching to avoid the temptation to look at it and to make sure you are attentive and locked-in when you need to be. The athletes deserve the coach's full attention the same way people in the audience deserve the clown's full attention.

So, if you ever get the opportunity to have lunch with a clown, do not miss out. You might learn a thing or two. They are the best in the business when it comes to optimal communication.

Be present. Be connected. Be attentive.

Act like a clown.

CHAPTER 21: WE

If you are Canadian, or simply a skiing fan, you probably know the name Mikaël Kingsbury. During the past decade, very few athletes have dominated their sport like this freestyle skier. His performances are almost superhuman. Take note of these numbers:

- 101 podium finishes in 120 World Cup starts (71 wins)
- 11 podium finishes in 12 world championship events (6 wins)
- 3 Olympic medals (2 silver and 1 gold)
- 9 Crystal Globe wins as the overall World Cup season leader

No wonder they call him the King. Many sports enthusiasts consider Kingsbury to currently be the most dominant athlete in the world.

When you succeed in your sport as much as he has, the pressure to perform optimally on demand is constant. Your entourage expects nothing but the best, all the time. You just cannot afford to fail. For an athlete of his stature, finishing second is not winning a silver medal, it is losing the gold medal.

Because of his domination, popularity and easygoing personality, Mikaël is a media favourite. Over the four-year Olympic cycle, he was one of Canada's top medal hopes heading towards the 2018 Games. As you can imagine, this meant doing hundreds of interviews and making many public appearances. At the time, the only significant accomplishment that was missing in his trophy case was that precious Olympic gold medal. It was no secret that Kingsbury was expected to win gold, and almost every reporter made sure to remind him of it.

"Mikaël, you've won just about every award in your sport. You are the heavy favourite to win at the Olympics. You finished second during the 2014 Sochi Games. Wanting to redeem yourself is certainly on your mind. How will you manage the pressure to win Olympic gold in PyeongChang?"

In other words, *You'd better win or you're a failure.*

Can you imagine having to face those questions, over and over again, without letting it get inside your head? Not an easy task, right?

So, what is the best way to manage questions like these?

For starters, athletes can distribute some of the pressure by focusing on the process. The athlete should avoid speaking about the actual result — we cannot stress this enough — because there are so many factors that can determine the outcome of a competition: The weather. The competitors. The environment. Realistically, nobody can control the end result. Having a result-oriented focus adds extra negative pressure. It can feel threatening.

Talking about your preparation, however, is putting the attention on several aspects that are fully within an athlete's control:

- The workouts in the gym
- The conversations with the coaches
- The simulations to help deal with nerves
- The extra hours of homework and video analysis to perfect technical and tactical elements

- The processes and routines to channel focus
- The rest and recovery to show up energized and excited to perform

These are all fundamental elements that are based on well-thought-out goals that are associated with fostering growth and development, and reaching excellence — elements that athletes will execute to get better. Thinking and talking about these factors can solidify one's mental strength — they act as reminders of important trainable pieces of the puzzle that, when executed properly, increase the probability of tapping into one's full potential.

Mikaël managed the press beautifully. He never fell into the "I will win gold" trap. When asked about the gold medal, he kept speaking about the work that needed to be done to become as ready as he could be to perform at his best. His comments when answering the reporter's questions came across as sincere, with bulletproof-type confidence.

Putting focus on the process is extremely beneficial for sports teams as well. Years ago, an NHL hockey team used wagons as a metaphor to break down the path to winning the Stanley Cup. The team focused entirely on adding a wagon to the train (each wagon represented a win) instead of focusing on the end goal (the Stanley Cup). One wagon at a time was one game at a time. The team needed 16 wins to win the championship. At some point, the team had 15 wagons stuck on the wall in the locker room, and the mentality was to win just one more wagon (process) instead of "We *must* win this game" (result).

Back to Kingsbury. To manage the press expertly, there was one more minor detail that needed to be polished — his usage of the word "I." Given that mogul skiing is an individual sport, athletes have a natural tendency to take everything on their own shoulders, a habit that is common across all individual sports: I will train very hard; I will do my homework; I will come up with solutions to setbacks; I will do whatever it takes to get better; I will make sure I'm ready.

When we use the word "I," we indicate that we are alone, single, solitary, solo. We send a message to our brain that we must manage everything by ourselves. The word "I" is often used subconsciously, out of habit, because we are not playing a team sport. However, this type of messaging can become hefty and substantial. We must be careful.

As Mikaël's mental performance coach, I wanted to bring this tendency to his attention. Over time, I collected many of the mogul skier's interviews and articles published in the press. During one of our one-on-one sessions, I shared a compilation of short snippets with Kingsbury, strategically put together so that it became obvious that the word "I" was being used over and over again.

"Are you noticing anything?" I asked.

"Yeah, I use the word 'I' a lot," he replied quickly. "I need to change that."

"Don't feel bad. Most individual-sport athletes fall into the same trap. Remember, you are not going to the Olympic Games by yourself. You have a team with you!"

I then walked up to the whiteboard, wrote "Mikaël Kingsbury" and proceeded to write the name of every individual who would be there, with him, at the 2018 PyeongChang Olympic Games:

- mogul skiing coaches
- jumping coach
- mental performance coach
- strength and conditioning coach
- agent
- physiotherapist
- team doctor
- massage therapist

- biomechanist
- team high-performance director
- parents

This team of 14 individuals shared a common purpose: to help him win the gold medal. Mikaël whipped out his phone and took a picture of what lay before his eyes.

"I will remember my team every time I think about the Olympic Games. In the media, I will use the word 'we' instead of 'I.'"

From then on, Mikaël rarely used the word "I" with the press. It became "we will work hard in the gym," "we will do our homework," "we will come up with solutions," "we will do whatever it takes to get better" and "we will make sure to be ready."

Using the word "we" allows the athlete to redistribute and delegate the pressure. It reduces anxiety. It reminds the athlete that they are not alone, even if they compete in individual sports. And that is exactly the effect it had on Mikaël Kingsbury heading into the 2018 Olympic Games. He felt supported. He felt surrounded. He felt like he had the right individuals in his corner to help him achieve his lifelong dream.

Fast-forward to Monday, February 12, 2018. It's 10 a.m. in South Korea. While Mikaël was rolling out of bed (yes, he is a great sleeper), his entire crew was having a meeting without him in the Team Canada building to discuss the mogul skiing competition coming up later that evening. Given the hype of the moment, the high-performance director Marc-André Moreau ran through all the details, step-by-step, to make sure everyone was clear on their roles and responsibilities. Better to be sure than sorry. To conclude the meeting, he opened the floor for any additional questions or comments. I shared some final words of wisdom as key reminders for everyone in the room.

"Every one of you in this room has played a critical role in Mikaël's success over the past years. He relies a lot on you. He

You're
part of
the team
even when
you're
alone.

truly believes in his team. But our job is not done. We must be at our best tonight if we want him to win.

"It's the Olympic Games, so Mikaël will be nervous. He will need us. We don't know when exactly, but he will certainly turn to us for comfort and support. We must remain calm, confident and positive all night, the same way we've acted during all those World Cup and world championship events. Don't do more, don't do less. Just do what you usually do because that's what Mikaël is expecting."

What unfolded that night in South Korea was spectacular. It was a demonstration of a group of coaches that worked together, purposefully, to help the King reach the top. The coaches were calm, cool and collected all night. Their body language demonstrated positivity and self-assurance. Mikaël Kingsbury's team was in full control.

In mogul skiing, the skier must execute a top-16-worthy performance to make it to the second round, and then perform a top-6 finish in the second round to make it to the third and final round, where they compete for a medal. In essence, the goal is simply making it to the next round, every round, because once in the final round, anything is possible.

Over the years, the coaches were used to witnessing Kingsbury finish first almost every round. Anything other than finishing first, or maybe second, was unusual. With the additional nerves to manage, Kingsbury finished fourth in the first round and second in the second round, which qualified him for the medal round, but in an atypical way — his coaches never flinched.

Mikaël went through his pre-performance routine, as usual, fist-pumping the coaches who were with him on top of the course. Locked in and totally focused, he propelled himself into the bumps and ended up ripping the course, performing a flawless and perfectly executed run to achieve his first Olympic gold medal.

You might think that the difference between using "me" and "we" is subtle. After all, visually it is only about flipping the m over so it becomes a w. But never forget that the brain believes what it hears, and we will always outweigh *me*. The difference is, in fact, very significant.

This story clearly demonstrates how powerful it is for an athlete to believe in their team. It is true for Kingsbury but it is also true for you, the coach. As a leader, you are never alone. Include your assistants. Call up your mentors. Think about all the staff around you. When you talk about the team, use "we." Not only will your stress level diminish, but you will also undertake pressure situations with more clarity and confidence.

CHAPTER 22: TOGETHER

In 1519, the Spanish explorer and conquistador Hernán Cortés arrived in Veracruz, Mexico, with more than 600 men, searching for wealthy treasures. Despite having a large crew, Cortés knew that his army would be outnumbered by the powerful Aztec empire, who were also better armed. To win the battle and ultimately conquer the land, Cortés needed to find a creative strategy to convince his men to "buy in" and become fully committed to the mission.

He ordered his men to burn the ships.

His army thought their leader had become a lunatic; his strategy was nothing short of crazy. But Cortés knew exactly what kind of effect his order would have. By getting rid of the ships, there was no turning back. The message was simple and clear: we succeed or we go down fighting.

Cortés's strategy worked.

With no exit plan, his men had no choice but to come together, become fully invested and work as a team, or else they were doomed. Their grittiness got the job done. Two years later, victory was declared.

This particular anecdote inspired me to be innovative over the years when it comes to building team chemistry. We do not recommend burning things down to inspire your team; however, we do encourage using methods that are out of the ordinary.

Below are three examples of activities I came up with to foster team cohesion.

PRACTISE HOW TO WIN

The thrill of victory and the feelings that come with it stay fixed in an athlete's memory. But if winning represents the sort of emotion that players dream of experiencing and that brings teams together, why not practise how to do it?

When I first started with the Canadian national women's baseball team, we played in a tournament in Japan as preparation for the world championships, which were taking place in Canada. We ended the tournament with a heartbreaking loss in the semi-finals. When we left Japan, we were deflated and demoralized.

Upon our return to Canada, I organized a series of games against some men's teams in Alberta. I figured facing tougher competition would make our task easier during the World Cup. I had forgotten a very important element, however: the joy of tasting victory. In those five tune-up games, we were winless with a 0–5 record. These were crushing defeats! We did not come close to winning any of the games. You could cut the tension among our team members with a knife; criticism came from every direction.

Fast-forward to our first game of the world championships tournament: a loss to Japan. It had now been more than 10 days since our team had tasted victory. We needed to change the tone and experience something positive. Since we had no game scheduled the following day, I thought we had to try something different at practice.

The next day, there we stood. With about 30 minutes remaining in practice and the Americans — our next opponent — waiting to take the field for their practice, I called our team together.

"I know it's been over 10 days since we've won a game. Let's just try to win this practice." The players and coaches stared at me as if I were from a different planet. I could tell what they were thinking just by looking at them. *What's he talking about? Win a practice? That's impossible!*

I instructed the players, "When your name is called, I want you to take a bat and a helmet and head to home plate. You will be the only one on the field. I want you to pretend you hit the ball and drive in the game-winning run that gives us the gold medal. You're the hero of the game and we want to see you celebrate." More confused looks. "We'll start with the lowest uniform number and work our way up. Number 2, you're up."

With great hesitation, she walked up to the plate and went through her hitting motion. Appearing unsure, she ran to first base with her arms up towards the sky, nothing fancy. "Well *that* seemed to be a memorable moment," I said with sarcasm, indicating I wanted to see more. "From now on, the coaches will grade your celebration from 1 to 10. The better your celebration, the better your rating."

That is when the magic set in.

The team went wild in the dugout — joy overcame everyone. When the last player took her turn, the rest of the team jumped on the field and rushed towards her at home plate to celebrate together. I had goosebumps. Looking at us, I am sure the Americans thought something along the lines of, *Canadians sure are crazy!*

Towards the end of the game the next day, facing our neighbours to the south, we found ourselves with a runner on second base and two outs. The stadium was packed with over 6,000 fans. It is at that moment I remembered our exercise at practice.

"It's all right. We went over this yesterday!" yelled a player next to me in the dugout. What was supposed to happen did, and for the first time in over 10 days, we were back on the winning track with a spectacular 2–1 victory against our archrivals. Our team finished first in round-robin play and ended up on the podium for the first time in the team's history. The experience strengthened the bonds between team members and restored a happy and winning environment. Our celebration drill at practice altered the psyche of our group, helping our players believe in themselves while creating a collective confidence heading into an important matchup against the Americans.

IMPROVISED MOVIE THEATRE

When planning for a world championship tournament held in Canada, I need to map out preparations for the three to four months prior to the event. Additionally, I welcome our players to the host city two weeks before the competition. This gives us an opportunity to train and practice on the field that will be used for the championship. Such an advantage should never be taken for granted.

Tournaments like these require the athletes to be away from their families and friends for several weeks. For one of these tournaments, without the players' knowledge, I contacted their loved ones and asked them to make a short video message of encouragement and motivation for their respective player. All of the families took part and gave me plenty of good material to review and put together as one big montage. The final product was a 45-minute video that included action highlights of each player along with their personalized well wishes. I kept this entire operation top secret, instructing my closest aides to keep quiet and to play along with the mission. Not even my assistant coaches knew what was happening.

On a scheduled day off, I asked my assistant coaches to help set up a hotel meeting room, transforming it into a movie theatre. Everyone pitched in, even though they were not sure what was happening! Everything was in order — admission ticket, decorations, giant screen and popcorn. I left no stone unturned.

Once the players were seated in the theatre, I presented myself in front of the group to welcome everyone and invited them to enjoy the performance. The lights went out and the video began. After a brief introduction, the first player's highlights were shown. Then, the personal message followed with greetings from her loved ones back home. The room became silent: you could hear a pin drop. The players slowly came to realize that each of them would be getting such a message. I even heard one player whisper, "I wonder who's in my part of the video."

Once the presentation was over and the lights came on, three quarters of the players were in tears. One player asked if we could watch it again, prompting the rest of the group to echo the request.

This unforgettable video had a direct impact on team morale. No matter what your team's level is, such an activity is possible. The idea behind it is to capture all the great moments of the season to create a highlight package that will motivate and inspire your troops at just the right time, as well as remind them they have cheerleaders in their family and friends. Your players will feel an unbreakable bond. Mission accomplished! Here are some guidelines to follow:

Start from the Very Beginning
Collect highlights tracing back to the very start of your season to present the entire journey.

Enlist the Help of a Parent or Another Volunteer

With everything else happening in a season, you probably won't have the time to do this yourself, so ask for help. You don't need fancy or expensive equipment. Today's smartphones come with more than adequate cameras for this project. Modern computers are also equipped with suitable editing programs to help you compile the final video product, including adding a soundtrack to the video.

Make Sure to Include Everyone

If your intent is to have an impact on your entire group and if you want everyone to feel part of the team, do not leave anyone out. Every member should be featured in the video as equally as possible.

Identify the Purpose of the Video

You want to light a fire with your team? Include some great training music as the background to your highlight pictures. Aiming to spark some emotions? Why not select pictures and moments that portrayed your team members' personalities? Have you been on the road for a while, away from loved ones? Feel free to include a personal video message from each team member's family and friends. This might require more time and effort since you want to preserve the element of surprise, but the emotional effect will be well worth it.

THE ADVENTURE

There are some TV game shows known for their teamwork components. For example, *The Amazing Race* spotlights 10 pairs of individuals taking part in a crazy adventure around the world.

Unexpected,
fun
experiences
**ignite
chemistry.**

Teams must find and solve clues by successfully completing obstacles of both a physical and mental variety. At the end of each stage, the last team to finish could be eliminated. This type of adventure can certainly be implemented on a smaller scale. You do not need to hop on an airplane and travel the world to create this experience. You do not need to feature the prospect of elimination, either.

During a tournament in Japan and with the help of some colleagues, I organized a similar scavenger hunt challenge in the city where we were staying. Our team was split into 10 pairs, each required to complete a series of obstacles, such as solving a Japanese puzzle, finding clues in a surf shop or locating hidden objects. The goal of the activity was to complete all tasks as quickly as possible. Organizing everything was quite an ordeal but thanks to the staff working together, it all turned out great — so much so that I have since run the same program many times. Players still rave about it many years later. If you are looking for a team-bonding adventure, this one will work wonders.

You could also stay local, using nearby facilities, equipment and staff resources. During a stay in Edmonton, the military base kindly organized a day of team building for our squad. Imagine participating in a shooting simulation, a fire rescue, tank rides through an Afghan village replica with real military members who served for Canada and an introduction to helicopter operation. Talk about a day filled with education, communication, competition and collaboration: all core elements of teamwork.

The key to success lies in your creativity and desire to provide an enjoyable environment for your athletes. Without realizing it, you will have the opportunity to get to know your players' personalities and to foster long-lasting ties between your team members. Do not be afraid to try something different or break from tradition. It is this type of out-of-the-ordinary experience that will stay engraved in the minds of your group forever.

CHAPTER 23: EXTRA MILE

At the age of 22, I decided to host my parents for dinner. At the time, I was a university student studying kinesiology, before specializing in sport psychology. Like most undergraduates, I kept my meals plain and simple. Cooking was not my forte.

Like any first experience that truly matters, I wanted to impress my folks, especially my mother. She was not a chef per se, but her cooking skills were impressive. While I was growing up, she kept me happy by filling my belly up with delicious, traditional, home-cooked meals.

As someone who likes to please others, I wanted this dinner party to be perfect. It was my way of saying thank you for all those years she'd spent in the kitchen when I lived at home. Needless to say, having my parents over for dinner was going to be a stressful experience. The pressure was on.

During the big day, I was adding the final spices to the spaghetti sauce when I suddenly realized that some vegetables were missing for the entrée. I also needed to buy some fruit for the chocolate fondue. I looked up at the clock: 4:00 p.m. My parents were scheduled to show up an hour later. The grocery store was around the corner, so I had plenty of time to grab the last items needed to complete my three-course meal.

I laced up my shoes and grabbed my backpack. As I walked out of the house, I was bewildered to see my parents walking up the front steps. Their errands hadn't taken as long as they'd thought they would, so they'd decided to surprise me. They were surprised to see me leaving just as they were arriving, and I explained that I was missing a few items for dinner and wouldn't be long. My authoritarian father told me to make it fast, and I didn't want to disappoint him, so I told them to make themselves at home and I'd be right back.

Rushing out of the house, I had one goal in mind: to be in and out of the supermarket in a flash so I could get back home as soon as possible to host my parents.

Most supermarkets are organized the same way: The first section is the produce area, which boasts different fruit and vegetable options. A little farther back are the deli and bakery. Along the external walls are the dairy products and various meats. Multiple aisles fill up the middle section with packaged and canned products.

In theory, the shopping excursion was deemed to be short. Walk in, grab the items, rush to the cash register and head out the door.

As I was picking out the best-looking apples, an elderly man walked up to me and asked for help. I had seen him at the store before, and he had always seemed a little strange to me, like someone who was better to avoid. As I saw him coming towards me, my immediate thought was, *Aw man, not him! I need to get back home, ASAP!*

I took five seconds to give the man direct instructions: "Go to aisle 5, walk halfway down the aisle and the peanut butter will be on the left-hand side."

The man thanked me and moved away slowly, beginning his long journey towards aisle 5. Meanwhile, I was zigzagging from table to table, selecting the fruits and vegetables I needed. As I was walking to the cash register, I glanced across the store and noticed that the man had taken a wrong turn and was lost in the bakery section.

At first, I selfishly told myself, *Forget him, he'll be fine, someone else will help him, you've got to get home quickly.* Then, an internal desire to help halted my march and jolted another thought: *JF, would you relax and just help the poor man? What is two extra minutes of your time going to change in your life?*

I walked across the produce area into the bakery section to reconnect with him. His wrinkled face was filled with enthusiasm.

"Hello, son! It's so nice to see you. Thanks again for your help. I'm almost there!"

Clearly, he was not. He was lost.

What struck me was how happy the man was to see me again. I could not believe how a simple gesture that lasted five seconds during my apple picking could have gone such a long way. Suddenly, I felt completely invested. Deep inside, I was committed and devoted to helping the old man. Within a split second, I forgot that my parents were waiting at home.

"You won't find the peanut butter here. Follow me, I'll take you to it."

What was supposed to take 2 minutes turned into 20. At a snail-like pace, we walked out of the bakery section, strolled past several aisles, marched halfway down aisle 5 and finally arrived at the peanut butter section. I happened to be enrolled in a sports nutrition class at the time, so I took the opportunity to explain the nutritional facts for every kind of peanut butter — creamy, crunchy, natural, sweet, mixed with chocolate, etc. The old man ended up choosing the Skippy brand, regular-sized and extra-crunchy. I took it down from the shelf and put it down into the small basket that was perched on the man's walker.

As I was letting go of the plastic jar, the old man grabbed my forearm and looked me straight in the eyes.

"Where are your parents?"

Surprised, I wondered, *How does he know my parents are in town?* "Why do you ask?" I asked nervously.

With soft eyes and a calm voice, he said, "I've been shopping here for the past 15 years. Never has someone helped me like you just did. I want to tell your parents that they did a great job raising a polite, thoughtful and caring human being."

Minutes later, I finally made it back home. As I walked through the door, my parents asked me why it had taken so long.

"Oh, do I have a story for you!"

Sometimes the most important life lessons happen during the least expected moments. That afternoon confirmed two things for me. First, becoming a coach was definitely the right career path. Impacting someone's life positively is both rewarding and fun. But the most important lesson was realizing that offering just a tad more of my time, effort and energy can become extremely meaningful. Small gestures show that you care and they can really go a long way.

In today's society, we do everything in a rush: We answer emails on the go. We use GPS systems to arrive quickly at our destination. We keep phone calls as short as possible. We run to get from one meeting to the other. We use abbreviations when we text with friends and colleagues. As we do one task, we think about the next one.

Even if you live a busy lifestyle, remember that doing a little more usually ends up being greatly appreciated.

As a keynote speaker, I always take some additional time to customize my presentations. Recently, I wrote a 90-minute speech for a Canadian Government ministry, based on their core behavioural values but combined and intertwined with mental performance principles and gold medal stories. The extra effort paid off — they loved it. As a speaker, I do not *have* to go the extra mile. I am not *asked* to do it. I *choose* to do it.

Do
a little
more,
get
a lot
more.

As a baseball coach, André regularly takes time to connect with players and staff, checking in just to see how they are doing. As a result, he has become a trusted leader.

When I travel the world for sports competitions, I will research the area ahead of time to make sure the athletes have what they need: locating the nearby restaurants, figuring out how to travel from the hotel to the competition venue, getting access to training schedules or or where to find them coffee. These additional efforts are not part of my job description, but in the end, it makes things a little easier on them and they appreciate it.

To build trust and chemistry, doing just a little more does not go unnoticed, so we want you to think about your behaviour with your athletes and teams. What can you do, just a tad more, that could go a long way? Could you:

- ... offer five additional minutes after practice to help an athlete perfect their technical skills?
- ... reach out more to athletes (a quick text, email or phone call) to learn about their current state, like "Hey! How are you doing? Thinking of you!"?
- ... delay your next meeting to offer just a few more minutes to someone who needs to share a concern with you?
- ... offer an additional positive comment when someone is down?
- ... do something totally unexpected, like sending a handwritten letter by mail?

Our suggestion is to offer a tad more, every day. See it as an investment — a few minutes of time in exchange for making someone's day a little brighter or easier. Never ever underestimate the power of small gestures.

A month after hosting my parents (dinner went well, by the way), I bumped into the same elderly man at the grocery store. He was so excited to see me again. With a trembling voice and a smile from ear to ear, he insisted on paying for my groceries. For a student living on a low budget, the kind gesture was greatly appreciated.

At the grocery store, like in sport teams, when you go the extra mile for someone, that someone will go the extra mile for you. There's nothing better for team chemistry.

SECTION 4

COORDINATION

IMPLEMENTING GROUND RULES,
MANAGING CRITICAL SITUATIONS AND
DOING THINGS DIFFERENTLY

CHAPTER 24: BLACK BOX

What was supposed to be a routine flight turned into a catastrophe on June 1, 2009. Air France Flight 447 was preparing for its departure at 10:34 a.m. from Rio de Janeiro in Brazil to Charles de Gaulle Airport in Paris. At 10:29 a.m. local time, everything was in place for the Airbus 330 plane to take off with 228 passengers and flight crew on board.

About three hours after take-off, a severe thunderstorm caused major turbulence. As the plane was flying over the Atlantic Ocean at an altitude of roughly 38,000 feet, communication between the cockpit and air traffic control was interrupted. The plane dove into the ocean, killing everyone aboard. Several days later, pieces of the Airbus were spotted floating on the surface of the ocean, but the rest of the plane and all the bodies of the victims were nowhere to be found.

After a plane crash, workers rush to find the precious black boxes. These two boxes are protected to survive impact, fire and water immersion. The first box will indicate the flight coordinates of an airplane at the time of the accident to help determine its cause. The second will provide audio of cockpit noises, any alarm sounds and conversations between pilots. This information is crucial in deciphering reasons and factors that cause a crash.

Upon the discovery of the black boxes on May 16, 2011, nearly two years after the Air France tragedy, it was concluded that incorrect and late reactions by the pilots led to a loss of plane control that continued until impact. According to the data, an overdependence on the autopilot computer system was the cause. The accident prompted aeronautic giants Boeing and Airbus to change certain protocols and permit pilots to fly their planes manually, regardless of what the autopilot system may suggest. These new practices are still in place today.

It sometimes takes a crisis to address a problem that has existed for a long time but has gone unnoticed or ignored. The lasting reliability of an airplane based on years of success in the skies led to the experts being blind to the potential for an eventual catastrophe.

Five years after the crash, on June 12, 2014, Team Brazil pulled off a brilliant 3–1 victory against Croatia in the opening game of the 20th FIFA World Cup. The tournament was held in Brazil and featured the top 32 soccer nations from around the globe. In the mecca of soccer, Brazilian national team members dreamed of capturing a world championship in front of their home fans. With young star player Neymar in the lineup, everything seemed possible.

Brazil finished in first place in Group A and followed up with wins against Chile in the round of 16 and Colombia in the quarterfinals. The next match would come against Germany in the semifinals — the final step before the grand finale, held in the mythical Maracanã Stadium in Rio de Janeiro. The Germans opened the scoring after only 11 minutes to take a 1–0 lead. They would then score four more unanswered goals before halftime for a commanding 5–0 lead. Never was this seen before! Brazil went on to lose the match 7–1 in front of a home crowd that was furious over such a poor performance. While Germany won the final to claim the World Cup trophy, Brazil finished the tournament in fourth place, thanks to a 3–0 loss at the hands of the Netherlands in the bronze medal game.

Following the match against Germany, the Brazilian media used their platform to display the public's disgust. Daily newspapers ran scathing headlines — "Worst Shame in History!", "A Historical Humiliation!" and "Brazil Demolished." Even the international sports magazine *L'Équipe de France* added its own opinion piece, titled "Disaster."

Over the next few weeks, the Brazilian soccer federation opened its national team's "black box" in an effort to uncover clues to explain the uncharacteristic embarrassment. At a press conference, the federation announced that the head coach had resigned and was being replaced by Dunga, who'd previously coached the national program after having captained the squad during his playing days. The federation's leadership vowed to review current practice methods, to evaluate the entire structure and to call upon experts from outside the organization, ensuring such a failure would never happen again.

Much like Air France's success prior to the plane crash, Brazil's rich and triumphant soccer history had rendered the country's soccer system complacent. Given so many incredible achievements in the past, it was unthinkable the team could ever lose in front of its home crowd.

The gravity of these two events is clearly very different. The loss of a soccer match is not at all similar to the loss of 228 lives. However, in both cases, it took a crisis to uncover new ways of doing things. Many sports teams wait for a crisis before taking action. We invite you to open your black box today before it is too late.

The Japanese use the word *kaizen* (which means "change for the better") to describe the philosophy of always looking for a better way, even when they believe they have found a recipe for success. The Japanese automobile manufacturer Toyota created an assembly line so efficient that a movement known as "The Toyota Way" is now employed by many enterprises worldwide. The approach has different objectives, such as increasing efficiency while evaluating overproduction, excess inventory and manufacturing defects. This means they are always ready to open their metaphorical black box for inspection or technical assessment. Such a business model compels the company to always be open to change and to try new ideas to optimize performance. This strategy is the foundation of Toyota's success.

Some questions can certainly arise from this philosophy when we are considering this approach for a sports team. How can we constantly evaluate ourselves in order to discover what works best and what needs improvement to help us get to the next level? After all, as the saying goes, "What got us *here* won't get us *there*."

To help incorporate the concept of a black box into managing your team operations, we propose the following suggestions:

OPEN THE BOX

It is time to put your cards on the table. The team needs to take a hard look at itself to see if all the pieces are in place for achieving its desired goals. It is time to ask the tough questions and address any elephants in the room — you know, the subjects no one wants to mention or talk about. In my role as a mental performance coach, I have worked with many sports organizations to help them open their black box. This can sometimes bring about some uncomfortable moments where group members feel very vulnerable. However, this step is essential in conducting a genuine examination of the state of the team and to help you compare the team's strengths and weaknesses to those of your competition. Be sure to involve the staff as well as the athletes in this activity. Feedback from the athletes can help you get the pulse of your group, offering a clearer picture of what works and what does not work for the team.

ANALYZE THE DATA

Once the state of the team is apparent from opening the black box, it is vital to assess the information revealed. There are plenty of things you'll need to consider, such as:

- Are the statistics helpful at all? For example, time of possession.
- Are athletes' training tests showing anything that can improve performance? For example, a beep test or vertical jump.
- Does any data confirm a team's recent success or failure? For example, the total number of players drafted by the organization.
- What are the keys to achieving a team's peak performance? For example, offensive or defensive skills.
- Do your collective goals confirm whether the team is heading in the right direction? For example, winning key games during the season.
- Is your sports science knowledge up to date? For example, use of neuro-biofeedback.

This step helps you understand if your black box is measuring the right indicators. Today's technology — smartphones, tablets, specialized cameras and coaching software — are seemingly limitless with their capabilities and allow you to obtain information that can help you draw certain conclusions and make any necessary changes. The best teams are those that use performance indicators to successfully determine their next course of action.

During the Women's Baseball World Cup in 2006, the Canadian national team experienced the exhilaration of beating Japan, the best team in the world, after a very competitive game. Everything went according to plan. The pre-game scouting analysis had been meticulous. Throughout the game, the players were always in the right spot defensively. It was as if André and the assistant coaches were mind readers, as they were able to anticipate every move the Japanese team would make. Two years later, Team Canada found itself facing that same Japanese team with the 2008 world championship on the line. Having won in 2006, the coaches planned to apply the same strategy and claim victory once again. After they reviewed scouting notes one last time, the game was underway. They quickly encountered a big surprise: the Japanese team was completely different, showing none of their tendencies from the last encounter. They had opened their black box and adapted accordingly. The Canadian coaches were beaten at their own game and it was too late to recover. They suffered a stinging loss but learned a valuable lesson.

SYSTEM REBOOT

After your analysis is completed, you must now reprogram your black box:

- What strategies will help execute your new plan?
- What equipment is needed to better measure performance indicators?
- Do you have the right personnel in place to carry out your mission?

- What can you learn from other groups that rely greatly on teamwork? For example, the army, an orchestra or firefighters.
- Is there anyone polluting the team environment that should be removed?

On one occasion, I supported the team leaders through the difficult decision to remove a star player from the team. This athlete was incredibly talented, but his attitude was very negative and was rubbing off on teammates. He was the bad apple in the bunch and was contaminating the team environment. The coaches were afraid that losing such a talent would leave a gaping hole. Despite all the coaches knowing this athlete had a negative impact on the team, nobody dared to mention it. It was only through opening the black box that the elephant in the room was finally addressed. In the end, the coaching staff all agreed to let the player go. Following his departure, the team quickly realized they did not miss him at all. Team cohesion grew significantly, and over time, the team performed even better.

Ric Charlesworth, an Australian Olympic field hockey coach, had an interesting system reboot approach that led to consecutive Olympic titles with the women's national team. Following an Olympic cycle of four years that culminated in a gold medal at the 1996 Summer Games, he called his athletes together to share his plan: "Now that we've tasted Olympic gold, I imagine you all have intentions of returning to the team for another four years. However, in order to do that, you'll have to try out playing another position." You can imagine the players' shock.

The reason for this tactic was simple. In learning a new position, the athletes would develop a stronger appreciation for what is required to play a different role. This would help them better understand the realities and situations of other players on the field.

We
dare you
to open
your
black
box.

Plus, in the event of an injury, a player could easily take her teammate's position. This coach opened the black box and put a backup plan in place before it was too late.

FOLLOW UP

With a new system now in place, it is necessary to open your black box on a continual basis. You should not have to experience a crisis to take action. Always remember: your black box should be a constant work in progress because success comes to those who evaluate themselves regularly. Do not be like a company CEO who waits for the year-end financial statements before realizing bankruptcy looms.

Successful teams are never satisfied with the status quo. They also recognize that what may have worked five years ago likely will not today or, at the very least, it will be less effective. Consider your personal computer: do you think you would get very far today with a Windows 95 operating system? Too many teams still operate with a mindset from a previous era.

Change always brings about great discoveries. Deactivate the autopilot program whenever you feel you are losing control of your team's destiny. Doing so can help avoid catastrophe.

CHAPTER 25: CRISIS

Toronto. Summer 2010. We are at a training camp to prepare the women's national baseball team for the upcoming world championship taking place in Venezuela. I can feel the players' excitement and anxiety. It is normal for this stage of the process.

Following a team dinner, I call the players and staff together for a meeting. On the agenda is a hypothetical emergency plan for the upcoming championship tournament — it's time to ready the team for a series of "what if?" scenarios. At this point, Venezuela is a hostile environment with economic and political instability. On top of that, the country's homicidal death rate is among the highest in the world.

I open up with this: "In a few days, we will arrive in a country where we will encounter many distractions. The best teams are the ones that can anticipate such challenges and be prepared for them. So, I would like to set up our emergency action plan together. You will be placed in four groups of five people. The coaches will be split up among you. I would like each group to identify problems that could arise during our trip. Next, your task will be to come up with a strategy to address each of them."

The athletes and staff all get to work. Here are some of the potential problems they identify:

- Someone's luggage does not arrive at our destination.
- There is a lack of security at the stadium and hotel.
- A player has their gear stolen.
- There is a lack of food.
- A teammate has been kidnapped.
- A natural disaster takes place.

We share the ideas among the groups, and after some tweaking, we come up with a strong list of possible issues. After two hours of brainstorming and discussion, we create an equally impressive action plan and feel ready for our upcoming adventure. Evidently, certain to-do items included in our emergency strategy must be handled prior to departure. One of them was to contact the Canadian ambassador in Caracas to inform them of our trip and location. I manage to obtain the Canadian Embassy contact information, which helps me feel at ease about the journey.

When we land in Venezuela, the team quickly notices how tight security will be during our time there. We receive a police escort service from the bus at the airport and there is a non-stop armed police presence near our hotel, with no one allowed to exit the hotel unescorted. During a rare stop at a nearby grocery store, I fill my basket while accompanied by two military guards with machine guns. Our team has never experienced this before — it's a completely different world. We open the tournament with a huge victory over Australia, but only a few days later the tournament is interrupted by something that was not anticipated in our "what if?" plan.

We have just finished an awesome game against Taiwan and the players and coaches are super pumped. Our post-game celebration takes place on the field, as it always does after a win. Hong Kong and the Netherlands wait for us to leave before taking the field in preparation of their game.

Our team boards the bus and heads to the hotel for our post-game meal and some downtime. Some of the players ask if they can go to a mall in the afternoon. I grant the request as long as the team's safety is assured. Everything seems to be in place for a nice shopping outing.

For the coaches, though, we have a different schedule. We plan to stay at the hotel to catch the Japan-Cuba TV broadcast for a little scouting in advance of our head-to-head matchups later in the tournament.

After the game, I head down to the hotel lobby so I can walk to stretch my legs a bit. Suddenly, I see the Hong Kong team enter the hotel following their game. The players appear shocked, with many of them in tears. Seeing the commotion, I figure they were disappointed after losing a close game against the Dutch team. The head coach comes in and approaches me while crying, and tells me a horrific incident has happened: one of their players was shot in the leg during the game.

I am utterly speechless.

I am already thinking of our next steps as I head back to find our coaches and deliver the news. We are very concerned, knowing our players are out shopping in the city. As we had agreed to a one-hour window for the players' free time outside the bubble, I insist on being the one to meet them at the hotel entrance upon their return, not wanting them to learn of the news from anyone else.

When they arrive, I ensure that I exhibit a demeanour that displays confidence and strength, but I also need to show our players I am aware of how serious the situation is and assure them everything is under control. In light of the shooting, I also inform them the tournament is suspended until further notice.

I remind the team that no one should leave the hotel under any circumstance.

Next, I contact our ambassador, who heads to our hotel for an emergency meeting in order to reassure us. With the hotel so busy, the only available spot to meet is right in front of the elevator doors on our floor, one we had practically all to ourselves. Partway through our meeting, the elevator doors open. The Australian coach comes out and informs me they do not have an embassy based in Venezuela and so, under Commonwealth laws, we are responsible for taking care of them.

When it rains, it pours! I ask the coach to assemble their club and join our meeting. We then discuss our next steps and ask our players to reflect on whether they wish to continue playing in the tournament. Half our team — 9 out of 18 players — share the desire to return home.

It is at this point I remember a very important lesson I learned along the way in my career: never make any decisions based on emotions. When you give yourself extra time and avoid making rushed decisions, things tend to settle down.

The next morning, the coaches are summoned to an urgent meeting that includes Venezuela's military chief, who wants to bring a sense of calm and comfort to everyone.

During the meeting, the Hong Kong delegation announces they are pulling out of the tournament and heading home the next day. We also learn that the player who was shot is recovering well in hospital and is not considered to be in critical condition — an update that brings relief to everyone. In light of these events, the suggestion is made to move the tournament to Maracay, a city thought to be more secure.

We then share the new details with the rest of the team. After having some time to reflect individually, our players organize a team meeting without coaches or staff to discuss the situation.

Following the meeting, one player still expresses the desire to leave the tournament. Wanting to respect her wishes, we begin the process of arranging her departure, but some logistical problems arise, making it more practical for her to stay.

Before agreeing to the change of tournament venue, I ask the organizing committee to ensure our team's hotel location and accommodations are the same as those for the Cuban team. I know that, politically speaking, Cuba is an ally of Venezuela, so I figure the team will be treated very well. Our request is granted and my prediction proves to be true. The hotel and amenities are perfect, helping ease our team's mindset. Now, we can get back to focusing on the competition, knowing security and other measures have been appropriately addressed.

Canada's next game is scheduled against the host Venezuela, with an anticipated crowd of 15,000 fans. We are informed that security perimeters are in place at one and two kilometres around the stadium, with officials also stationed at the entrances. Upon our arrival at the stadium, it is evident our definition of secure is quite different from what is provided. People are walking into the stadium and setting off the metal detectors without anyone stopping them from entering.

You can feel the tension among the players during the pre-game warm-ups. Our starting pitcher's hands are shaking while she throws in the bullpen. Even my mind wanders a bit, with thoughts consumed by our team's and my own security. *What if what happened during the Hong Kong–Netherlands game occurs during ours?*

A baseball diamond is designed such that both teams have their respective dugout, or bench. Inside the dugout, we are sheltered and not very visible to the public. However, players and coaches do not have that luxury when out on the field, as they are fully exposed in front of many boisterous fans in an open stadium. Following baseball tradition, team managers gather at home plate with the umpire crew just before each game in order to exchange

All eyes
are on you;
what will
you do?

lineup cards. Now, for good reason, I am also a little fearful of being exposed. Of course, though, I must have courage and show the right example to our team.

This small act of heading out to the plate — often taken for granted — takes on a whole new level of significance now. Wanting to lighten the mood in order to reduce the pressure we are feeling, I look at one of our assistant coaches. Knowing he is just as worried and nervous as I am, I call him over.

"To help with your development, I want you to learn and practise as many of the head coach and managerial responsibilities as possible — including pre-game duties. So, I want *you* to do the lineup exchange today."

The team bursts out in laughter and my assistant coach sits back down on the bench, only now realizing that I was kidding. Coaches must know their teams, and I knew mine would benefit from a little joke at that exact moment. With a smile on my face, I jump on the field and head to home plate.

When facing a crisis, and to help keep your team together, coaches should consider the following points:

- In the midst of the storm, emotions can seem more important than they really are. Your brain's limbic system is on high alert, which can cause you to become impulsive and reactive. It is crucial to remain calm in order to properly reflect and make the right calls. So, give yourself some time. Remember the 24-hour rule. The dust will settle, and everything will fall into place. If not, you'll have a better mindset to plan a different strategy.
- It is pretty much guaranteed that, at some point, athletes will think as individuals instead of as

members of a team. This is normal. Remember, sticking to fundamentals keeps the foundation strong. Again, the brain's limbic system plays such a vital role. Coaches must remind their players that we are all in the same boat, vying for the same goal. Staying the course together will help us accomplish our mission.

- Healthy crisis management happens with honesty among the members of a group. Keeping secrets does no good for anyone. Coaches who are up front and transparent with their athletes and staff and show their team the proper respect they deserve will help earn the same in return.

- Before you mention a single word, athletes will look you in the eyes, see your face and notice your demeanour — even the way you walk. Show them the best version of your coaching self. Always present body language that exudes confidence and reassurance especially during a crisis situation..

- Setting the right tone can also help maintain control during emergencies. Coaches need to know when to be lighthearted and when to be serious. It is also necessary to show comfort in situations of discomfort. Sometimes we may ask ourselves, "What do I tell the athletes?" Believe in yourself and be natural. If you know your team, you will know what to say to them, as well as how and when to say it. (See chapter 17, "Get Personal," for more details.)

A crisis can be very serious, so we must treat it strategically with calmness and intelligence. If you can manage a crisis effectively and successfully, your team will be better equipped to respond if one occurs in the future. So, consider the experience as an investment.

Since that world championship tournament in 2010, devising a thorough and complete plan for a competition and any possible emergency scenarios has been a no-brainer for our coaching staff. Hurricane Dennis in Cuba in 2005 and an earthquake in Taiwan in 2006 also afforded our staff the experience to develop certain tools that allow us to better manage scary events today. While it may be necessary or beneficial to include your players in the process, nothing prevents you from creating a plan on your own or involving only your coaches and support staff. Whatever you decide, it is essential the plan limits any negative impact there could be on your team or on athlete performance.

A crisis is rarely predictable. But taking time to prepare for a crisis and to develop an emergency action plan will give you the confidence to address a situation when it arises, even if the details are unpredictable.

CHAPTER 26: ONE-ON-ONE

As leaders, having individual meetings periodically with athletes is essential to building trust and chemistry. In reality, most coaches are not meeting with athletes enough to consider each athlete's individual needs to help them tap into their full potential. Why? Most coaches tell me they simply do not have enough time for additional meetings. Well, our recommendation to you is simple: make the time.

Having some one-on-one time to assess, evaluate, brainstorm or simply check in is one of the most beneficial investments there is to build solid rapport between coaches and athletes. The content shared between two people can be completely different than if the same content was shared in front of a group. Because it is a safer environment, individuals tend to open up more and conversations become more authentic.

The setting for one-on-one conversations is very important to consider. As a mental performance coach, most athletes I work with are adults. The conversations happen in a professional environment where clients feel comfortable and safe. But when I meet with younger athletes, especially minors, I make sure a parent,

You don't
coach
a team;
**you coach
individuals**
who are
part of
a team.

guardian or coach is present as well to avoid being alone with the client. I follow a principle called "The Rule of Two," developed by the Coaching Association of Canada, that requires a third party to be present to protect athletes and coaches. The principle ensures that all interactions and communications remain open, observable and justifiable. (To learn more about the Rule of Two, take a look at this website: www.coach.ca.)

Next are 10 tips to help you get the most out of one-on-one sessions.

SAY THEIR NAME

"Hey. How was training today? Any lessons learned?" is not the same as "Matthew. How was training today, my friend? Did you take away any lessons learned?" The former is somewhat cold and objective while the latter is more personalized. Hearing our name grabs our attention a little more because it is part of our identity — "Oh, that is me!" It adds a personal touch.

Adding someone's name in a sentence may be a subtle change, but the effect is significant. There are specific neurological connections that fire off and make the person feel more acknowledged. The individual then becomes more attentive and, therefore, more connected with you.

Be careful, though, because overdoing it can cause some harm. Using somebody's name repetitively can be perceived as manipulative. When used just enough, hearing our name creates a positive internal buzz that demonstrates the other person actually cares about us.

SET THE ROOM CORRECTLY

Comfort is key to ensure quality conversations. For starters, if possible, avoid having a desk between you and the athlete. It creates a barrier. It is better to have a coffee table that is smaller and lower, or no table at all, to improve human energy flow. Consider using comfortable chairs, especially for longer meetings. Sitting uncomfortably can disrupt the flow of thoughts, which could hinder the conversation.

Offering something to drink can also improve a conversation — some coffee, a glass of water or a cup of tea. Sipping on a beverage tends to make the environment more informal, which enhances free-flowing conversations.

We also suggest using whiteboards to better explain content, specifically for visual learners. Sometimes a discussion can become abstract — like tactical plays, psychological constructs or detailed training plans — so illustrating your point can go a long way. As they say, a picture is worth a thousand words.

Lastly, having a clock up on the wall, strategically positioned so you can glance at it once in a while, is key to be mindful of time.

PUT YOUR PHONE AWAY

Even though this tip is self-explanatory, it deserves a special mention given how much smartphones can be detrimental during interactions. When vibrations, flashing lights and *dings* are going off, our attention is drawn to the electronic device like a Pavlovian dog. The phone wins every time. *Who is contacting me? I wonder who liked my last post. Did he return my email yet?*

Think about what you are indicating to the other person when you keep glancing at your phone: "My phone is more important than you."

The phone becomes a distraction if it is next to you. So, put it away. If your phone is placed in the drawer or left in another room, do not worry, emails and text messages will still come in.

Simply put, when your phone is put away, you optimize your concentration and enhance rapport with your athlete. Last we checked, robust chemistry is built through human interactions, not through technology.

MAKE THE CONVERSATION ENJOYABLE

Who were your favourite teachers of all time? What was so special about them? What made you like them so much?

Was it because they taught great theories? No! Did they speak with a monotonous voice? Of course not. Did they present PowerPoint slides filled with graphs and tables? We doubt it!

Your favourite teachers were energetic, passionate, funny, thought-provoking storytellers. They cared about the students. In the end, they made sure the learning environment was enjoyable. These same principles apply during one-on-one conversations.

Is it fun to be in a room with you? Are you great at putting people at ease? Are you good at breaking the ice to release some tension in the room?

Smiling will connect with others and attract attention. Cracking a smile, from time to time, can also relieve stiffness and awkwardness, especially during serious conversations.

When people enjoy spending time with you, chances are they will want to meet again in the future. Humour creates an enjoyable environment. When people receive positive emotions such as happiness, they are more engaged and retain more information.

One of the most important responsibilities we have as coaches is to teach, and when your presence is enjoyable, getting through to people becomes much easier.

USE BREATHING TECHNIQUES

Breathing mindfully for approximately one minute before getting into a one-on-one conversation is beneficial to flush whatever was on your mind, so you can become totally present and offer your full attention. You can also kick off a one-on-one meeting with a short meditation, so both of you will begin the session with a fresh start.

Using respiration during a one-on-one meeting is also beneficial. Connecting to your breath once in a while during the conversation is a great way to check in and activate your prefrontal cortex, the part of your brain that is responsible for active listening and information processing. Mindful breathing is also a great way to bring awareness to your posture. Proper body language is critical to improve communication. When you are sitting or standing, make sure you are not slouching or appearing disengaged. Nobody likes that.

SHOW THAT YOU CARE

Want to improve chemistry with someone? Get personal with them! (See chapter 17, "Get Personal," for more details.)

Ask how their family is doing. Inquire about other sports they play. Find out what they are studying at school. Ask questions about their life goals. Do not be too intrusive but ask just enough to show that you are genuinely interested in the person, not just the athlete.

When an athlete feels that you really care about them, they will go the extra mile for you. If you took this approach with every individual on the team, the athletes would be more likely to buy into your program, mission and vision.

HAVE A PLAN — 5/50/5

How can you make sure that a one-on-one meeting will be productive? Have a plan. Ideally, the plan for the meeting should be constructed with the athlete ahead of time so they become more engaged and invested in the meeting. (See chapter 10, "How Are You?", for more details.) When the plan is clear, both of you are mentally prepared to discuss the topics at hand. This also usually avoids any surprises.

Meetings should be no longer than 60 minutes. Your attention span will start to decrease if you go any longer. Have an agenda for the meeting. Use the first five minutes to set the tone, break the ice and identify the topics for discussion. The bulk of the meeting should not be longer than 50 minutes. Please, do not rush the conversation. Focus on having quality conversations instead of just scratching the surface.

The last five minutes are critical. Ask the athlete to summarize the main points that were discussed. That way, you can confirm if the topics you both covered were well understood. Also, highlight what needs to be put into practice and offer any additional homework if necessary.

Typically, a solid plan leads to a solid conversation. Like the saying goes, if you fail to plan, plan to fail.

USE PARAPHRASING

Paraphrasing means formulating someone else's ideas in your own words. Here is an example of how a coach might use paraphrasing when speaking to an athlete:

"To be clear, what you are saying is that you need to take some additional time off because you are tired?"

The importance of this communication skill is threefold:

1. the athlete becomes aware that you have acknowledged and understood what they said,
2. it validates (or not) that you understand their point of view and
3. if you did not understand correctly, the athlete can provide the correct information.

When used properly, paraphrasing fosters connection and trust.

TAKE NOTES

Loads of information is shared during a one-hour conversation. It is almost impossible to remember everything, especially if you are meeting individually with every athlete on your team. Document the information on a notepad or on your computer, so records are kept from those important conversations.

Note-taking also helps to bring topics from the previous conversation to the next one, for example:

"Were you able to rest properly last night? Did you like that Netflix documentary you mentioned you were going to check out? How did your test go last week?"

Athletes love it when you follow up on past conversations. It shows that you are making an effort to connect with them.

Carry a notepad with you. It is a lifesaver.

NEVER RUSH A DISCUSSION

We like to predict how long a discussion will last based on past conversations. Then, we subconsciously decide how much time it should take to address each topic during our next chat. Be mindful of this. Sometimes we decide to rush the discussion just so we can cover every point.

If you cover two out of four discussion points, but those two points needed to be addressed properly, that is perfectly fine. Make sure you go deep and cover all the angles. Usually, the benefits of covering more ground on fewer topics are greater than just skimming over everything. If you run out of time, don't worry — simply set up another meeting to tackle the remaining points.

Fitting individual meetings into our busy schedules can be a challenge, but it is never a waste of time. Making time for one-on-one meetings is an investment in your athletes. Using these 10 tips will help improve your conversations.

CHAPTER 27: HATCHET

It is the last day of the training camp: it's time to make the final decisions. Everyone gave it their all over the past few weeks and you are unsure who to release, but you can't keep them all. One athlete stood out with impressive skills but has a terrible attitude. Another athlete is a workhorse but is struggling to connect with some of the veteran players on the team.

You feel torn.

After considering all the pros and cons, your choices are finally made — the time has come to reveal who made the team. Because of your insecurity, you keep wondering how you will announce the big news. You end up choosing an easy way out. Inspired from sports movies, you ask the athletes to gather around and you tell them the following:

"There's a list pinned to the wall in the hallway. If your name is on the list, welcome to the team. If not, better luck next time."

The athletes rush out of the gym, hoping to see their name on the list. While some athletes are ecstatic, others are devastated because they did not make the cut. The area around the list becomes a complicated and awkward mixture of emotions: joy and sadness, happiness and frustration, cheers and tears, high-fives and pouting faces.

The list approach is entertaining for movie viewers, but in real life, there are better ways to manage this delicate moment. As coaches, it is your job to make the hatchet experience as constructive as possible for the athletes.

Rejection can lead to some of the most agonizing feelings a human being can experience. Ask anyone who got fired from a job, turned down for a bank loan or dumped for someone else — it is extremely painful and creates long-lasting effects. Getting released from a sports team is no different. Athletes feel worthless, useless, talentless and undesired. Neurologically, rejection triggers the same areas in our brain as when we experience physical pain. No wonder it hurts. Getting cut can leave deep psychological scars.

For coaches, having to release athletes is an unavoidable duty. Here are a few tips to make this process as smooth as possible.

BE EMPATHETIC

There is no empathy whatsoever shown by posting a list on a wall. Each athlete has willingly volunteered their time and effort for your sports program; the least you can do is offer some time to each one of them individually to explain your decision. The athlete deserves to know why they were released. Show that you care. Be attentive and respectful. Make sure to show empathy by acknowledging their feelings.

Because of the uniqueness of the moment, this meeting can actually become fulfilling for both the coach and the athlete. If suitable, let yourself be emotional as well. The athlete will respect your authenticity and empathy.

**The way
you cut
an athlete**
will define
who you are.

The athlete may require some additional time to digest the news, so do not rush the discussion. Offer the appropriate amount of time that is needed. If the conversation runs 10 minutes longer than expected, see it as time well spent.

Conclude the meeting with a firm handshake.

GET STRAIGHT TO THE POINT

After entering your office, the athlete has only one question in mind: *Did I make it or not?* Do not leave the athlete hanging. Too often, coaches will ramble on and on instead of just getting to the point. Dragging out the situation is quite common for coaches who are uncomfortable delivering the news.

Do yourself a favour: rip the Band-Aid off quickly and begin to deal with the aftershock immediately. Embrace the discomfort, avoid the suspense and get straight to the point. The athlete will most likely forget anything you said before hearing they were released, so it's no use expanding on details *before* delivering the news — do it after.

BE PREPARED

Athletes have the right to know why they got released. To justify your decision, come into the meeting ready to share reasons that are quantitative, with data and statistics, and qualitative, involving attitude and behaviours. Offering a detailed explanation can help the athlete move on and transition to something else. Make sure to highlight their strengths and compliment their play. They must leave with some positive feedback.

This meeting is an opportunity to share what they need to work on, like improving specific technical skills or adding muscle mass to become physically stronger. If the athlete shows interesting potential, you could also offer some opportunities to stay connected to the team. Perhaps they could play on the development team, or you could use them as an affiliated player that can be called up in certain situations. Maybe they could train with the team from time to time or be part of the taxi squad.

Showing the athlete that you have their interest at heart will have positive consequences in the long run.

SAY THANK YOU

Never underestimate the power of being polite with others. Be grateful and thankful every chance you get. When athletes pour their heart and soul into the hope of getting selected, the least you can do is thank them for coming out.

Showing gratitude will speak volumes about your standards and morals as a coach. Ending the meeting with the words "thank you" displays class and professionalism.

Keep in mind, as a coach, you are the face of the organization. Your behaviour represents the values of your team and club or organization. The athlete may not agree with your decision, but they will respect your genuineness if you acknowledge their participation.

TAKE RESPONSIBILITY

"I would have kept you on the team but the assistant coaches didn't agree with me. I'm sorry kid, I liked you." This is not fictional. We know athletes who, unfortunately, were told these exact words.

Having to release players can be a coach's nightmare. Nobody enjoys telling an athlete that they were not good enough. But please, do not find excuses. Never blame it on others. Take full responsibility and live with the consequences.

Do you ever get it wrong? Absolutely.

Will you second-guess your decisions? Possibly.

Will you regret your choices? Maybe.

Only the future will tell. But in the end, you are the boss, and you must accept and live with the good and the bad.

CONSIDER THE ENTRY AND EXIT

Getting released can be a shameful and embarrassing experience. The ego takes a major hit. When an athlete feels this way, the natural instinct is to hide. They certainly do not want to exhibit their distress in front of others. Because they are down, they do not want to witness players who made the team celebrating together — especially when they are no longer part of that tight group. That would be a double whammy. In moments like this, it is hard to find a way out without feeling totally ashamed.

When conducting tryout exit meetings, using a room with two doors is the best approach. This way, the athlete can enter through one door and leave the room through the other. This prevents any contact or interaction with other athletes. If using a room with two doors is not possible, I suggest that each athlete waits in a separate location until someone notifies them that it is their turn.

The higher the stakes, the greater the disappointment. For some athletes, getting cut from a national team program is more than not making a team. It is failing to reach a dream goal. As you can imagine, athletes can get quite emotional in these situations.

As I coach, I have never conducted these exit meetings alone. I have always been surrounded by assistant coaches or staff members. It gives me an unconscious support that is so important. Several years ago, I came up with the idea of setting up a safe space that was located near the exit door. In this space was our team business manager, Penny Fitzsimmons. Penny was also the unofficial team mom. Everyone loved her. Always smiley and cheerful, she cared deeply for the athletes.

This safe space helped the athletes deal with the moment of truth, discovering they didn't make the team, and prepare to return to normal life. In this room, athletes felt safe to express their emotions with Penny. In all cases, everything ended with support.

The joys of making a team and the sorrows of getting the hatchet are moments that stay with us forever. As a coach, making sure to be professional, respectful and authentic during this event should be prioritized. You never know what the future might bring your way.

Who knows, maybe:

- an athlete you released years ago becomes the mayor of your city and could back your program during hard times,
- an athlete who got the hatchet turns into a rich philanthropist who could donate funds to improve your athletic facilities or
- an athlete who got cut comes back to serve your program as a coach.

When you use the hatchet, please do it with compassion and professionalism.

Thank you. [Firm handshake]

CHAPTER 28: HASHTAG

Did you know that more than 23 billion text messages are sent worldwide each day, or that 66 percent of North Americans look at their cell phone at least 160 times per day? Clearly, technology dominates our lives.

This dependency is reflected equally in athletes today: they have developed a synergy with their phones. Take a walk through a university campus cafeteria or glance around a shopping mall and you will see the majority of young people have their eyes glued to their telephone screens. The world of sports is not immune to this phenomenon. As a coach, you will undoubtedly have to monitor or place controls on the athletes' use of personal electronic devices in order to build and protect a healthy team chemistry.

But be careful — if you think you will win the battle over the use of technology, you will surely lose. You have to take a new approach and think differently. Today's athletes communicate with one another every day through text messaging or social media. It is inevitable that you will miss certain information or conversations. If comments shared by the athletes are negative, there is a strong possibility they can affect the team. Here are some situations that could have a significant impact on the team.

For example, imagine two players texting each other privately after a game:

> Emma: I don't understand why Jessica is playing more than me.
>
> Sarah: She doesn't deserve to play! She does nothing on the court.
>
> Emma: And she's not a good teammate, either.
>
> Sarah: I don't like her, either.
>
> Emma: She always yells at us during games.
>
> Sarah: I know! It's just not fair!

This sort of talk happens far more often than we might think or care to believe. It only takes a few minutes before these two players add some other team members to the group chat and voilà — you have team turmoil on your hands. A conversation between two people could spiral into:

- A group chat that excludes several players from the team but talks about them in their absence
- FaceTime calls — that leave no record of the conversation — gossiping about players
- Cyberbullying against a team member using words and/or photos

One of the harmful effects of athletes' cell phone use is that they may lean toward impulsivenss instead of reflecting before acting. Thoughtful reflection helps us with many things, including:

- Mental preparation before a competition; for example, sitting quietly on a team bus when heading to the arena or stadium
- The ability to keep focused and stay in the moment during a practice or game, or during a time-out or break
- Critical-thinking and problem-solving skills, such as post-game analysis and self-reflection

If an athlete's phone is available before, during or after a competition, these thought-filled moments of reflection will be greatly compromised.

In addition, increased use of personal electronic devices can lead to a decrease in personal interaction among team members. While many chats could occur via different forms of technology, there is no real substitute for human interaction and live, personal conversation. In your role as coach, you will absolutely need to consider how phone use will be managed within your team.

There are certain times when it is particularly important to restrict phone use, and we discuss these below. We encourage you to consider them when developing your team policy concerning phone use, as they can be just as beneficial to team coaches and support staff as they can be to the athletes and, therefore, your overall success as a team.

TEAM MEALS

No phone use is to be permitted during team meals, no matter the location or the time. Team meals are considered a sacred opportunity for gathering together to encourage connection and bonding among athletes and staff. The time spent unwinding, conversing and entertaining is a privilege not to be compromised. Team members should be asked and expected to leave their electronic devices stored away during team meals.

PRACTICE AND GAME PREPARATION

We insist on cell phones being left in the locker room or in the athletes' gym bags during practices and competitions. Also, when travelling as a team, athletes and staff should deposit their phones into a box that will serve as a storage bank while on the bus. Everyone could benefit from this opportunity to reflect on individual and team performance. This is an opportunity for athletes to mentally prepare for the next competition.

BEFORE SLEEPING

It is highly recommended that use of phones and other electronics should end at least half an hour before going to bed. The blue light from the screen reduces the body's production of melatonin, the hormone that regulates your sleep cycle. This can make falling asleep and waking up very difficult. The content consumed through the use of phones, tablets or computers will also activate the brain, which needs to slow down in order to rest and get a good sleep. As an alternative, we suggest reading a book before falling asleep. To help resist the temptation to grab your personal electronic device, put it in a safe place out of reach. Do not forget that when one athlete has a night without substantial rest, it could impact other members of the team, while a rough night's sleep for *several* players will have negative effects on the entire team. As a rule of thumb, a team that sleeps well will be a team that performs well.

Too much
scrolling
leads to
fewer
connections.

We cannot talk about cell phones without mentioning social media. Whether it is Facebook, Twitter, Instagram, TikTok, Snapchat or any other platforms, the rapid rise in annual users is showing no signs of slowing down. For example, recent surveys show that some of these platforms report totals surpassing three billion users across the globe. Almost 58 percent of the world's population uses at least one form of social media, while this rate increases to 82 percent among those aged 13 and over in America. While some generations struggle mightily with this growing phenomenon, others have flourished. Like it or not, the use of social media has become part of our daily living. We need to accept this reality and work with it, not against it.

Keep in mind that the digital imprint left by social media will not disappear. One misstep shown in pictures or some choice words printed online can cost an individual or a team dearly. Today's society loves to judge people very quickly through what they post on social media.

There are many examples of people, some in high profile positions, who have spoken or written one sentence, one word of profanity or taken one inappropriate photo that ends up on social media, and all their previous positive moments and accomplishments are erased instantly in the eyes of the public, or even their employer.

Imagine you coach a basketball team. One of your players has posted on their Instagram account a picture of a scoreboard reading 85–35 with the hashtags #theysuck, #notevenclose and #suchadisgrace. A post of this kind can elicit a negative perception and a public reaction that would label your program #disrespectful and #unprofessional.

Do not take the risk. Be sure to stress key principles when developing a team policy on social media. This policy will help your team focus on standards of excellence. But everyone must board the ship: otherwise; you will surely drown. Whether the athlete has posted something inappropriate, or someone else has posted something about that athlete that puts them in a difficult and possibly controversial position, the repercussions of social media posts can haunt people for years.

Here are some suggestions to prevent a bad social media experience:

DRUGS AND ALCOHOL

Under no circumstances should any athlete, coach or support staff member be associated with any drugs or alcohol in print or photography — even if they are in a leisurely social setting. Your team and program reputations are at stake. If anyone affiliated with your team wishes to have a beer, there is no need to broadcast that on social media or even in public. Certainly, you should never share any pictures or video of an intoxicated athlete or staff member on the internet. Just imagine media outlets reporting pictures from Facebook of one of the players vomiting while wearing your team clothing. If you operate in a school environment, be aware of the institution's code of conduct.

CLOTHING

Athletes and coaches should consider their clothing selection before anything is published online. In certain situations or team members must wear clothes that identify an official sponsor. Since many sponsorship deals can be hard to acquire for teams or programs, athletes and staff should always recognize the effects of their clothing choices on future relationships with sponsors. It should also go without saying that there is no place for inappropriate outfits, exposed undergarments or nudity. In some cases, you represent not only your team but also your city, province or even country. Athletes and staff must always be mindful of this.

RESPECTFUL LANGUAGE

Athletes and team staff should always use language suitable for publication and public consumption. No matter the language spoken or typed, it is important that messages be socially acceptable and not contain any words or meanings that discriminate against race, religion, ethnicity, sexual orientation or any other distinction. If you find yourself unsure or hesitant of whether something should be posted, it is likely best not to post it at all. Like the expression goes, "Always think before you speak," or in this case, post. Remaining neutral will help avoid controversy.

OBTAINING PERMISSION

In order to avoid potential problems, make an effort to gain permission from any vested parties before posting on the internet. This is particularly important for opposing team members that may appear in the photos or videos. For example, during a welcoming meal organized by a tournament committee, your athletes may be excited and eager to celebrate the event by capturing moments that will forever solidify their memories. However, the others seen in the background never gave their consent to be included. There is never any harm in asking them for permission before you share publicly. In fact, such a gesture can show other teams your group's values and DNA.

SENSITIVE TEAM INFORMATION

The strategy for your upcoming game? An injury to one of the players? A new play or tactic introduced in practice? The starting lineup for your next game? No comment. Sharing sensitive team information on social media can only present challenges. Some members will even blame team losses on an individual who publicly reveals these secrets. As a coach, you definitely want to avoid any ways to break the bonds of a team, so it is important to know when and how to keep team information private.

Many options exist that can help create a team environment where all members can stay connected with one another through their devices. Apps like Slack and WhatsApp allow for athletes and staff to converse, share documents, post videos and much more. This kind of communication is a key ingredient when building team chemistry.

Never let technology ruin your team chemistry. If you ever feel outclassed or overwhelmed by technology, we encourage you to call a media specialist to speak to the team about proper phone and social media use.

And always remember that liking or sharing something someone else published can be equally damaging to what you publish yourself and can taint your public image. A good reputation is hard to create and keep — you would never want to lose it with one single post.

So be #wary and be #wise.

CHAPTER 29: GOAL GETTING

At the beginning of a new season, I conduct mental skills workshops to help sports teams build mental toughness. To kick off the meetings, I ask the players what the team goal is for the year. I get the same answer every time: win the league championship.

I typically fire back with, "That's great, but that's not very original. Doesn't *every* team in the league want to achieve the same goal?"

All players in the room nod their heads in agreement.

"That goal is too obvious; any team can come up with that. But the reality is, only one team can lift the trophy at the end of the year, and 19 other teams are competing for the same hardware. This makes winning a championship quite unique, doesn't it?"

The athletes agree again.

"Well, in that case, you must operate in a unique way to achieve something unique."

Winning a championship is only *what* you want to achieve. What really matters is understanding *how* you will achieve the *what*. Chances are, most teams will not put too much thought into this second step. If you identify *how* you will win and execute it well, then the team will become unique.

Setting
goals is
easy;
reaching
them
is **hard.**

This short speech seems to make sense to athletes and coaches when they hear the message I'm trying to convey. However, even though everyone gets it, few successfully put it into practice.

Why? Because reaching ambitious goals is a hard thing to do.

To reach year-end goals, you need a clear plan from the beginning, but more importantly, it is critical to have checkpoints during the season to evaluate the situation, measure progress, polish tactics and strategies, and apply changes when needed. Goal setting is one thing, but focusing on goal *getting* is what truly matters.

As a mental performance expert, I come back every month or so to review a team's progress. Sometimes, I must force coaches to think differently and adapt, especially if the team is not performing according to the plan at each of the checkpoints. As someone external to the team, I am not influenced by day-to-day details, so I come in with fresh eyes. Often, elements that must be adjusted are obvious to me. In a case like this, I provide advice — for example, offering ways to improve workouts and training sessions — so the team can get back on track according to their checkpoints. The meetings serve as monthly check-ups.

Below are some considerations we will discuss at these checkpoint meetings.

PRIORITIZE DAILY GOALS

Every time your team practises or competes is an opportunity to get better. Never let those opportunities go to waste. In order to achieve long-term goals, you must first meet established short-term ones. Too much attention is put on weekly, monthly and yearly goals, and not enough emphasis is placed on daily goals — or what I like to call "now" goals. What needs to be accomplished today? A team can only improve what they are currently working on.

You might argue that long-term goals are valuable to clarify the final destination and to give meaning to short-term goals. You are right. However, because long-term goals are off in the distance, athletes and coaches can easily lose sight of them. Plus, thinking about what is down the road can bring about uncertainties. The best way to manage uncertainties is by focusing on the certainties. What is going on now is more predictable, which reduces anxiety significantly and helps everyone focus.

Let's use driving a car at night as a metaphor. Your destination is several kilometres away, so you must focus on the road lit up by your headlights instead. To drive properly, it is not useful to look out in the dark. By relying only on what the headlights are illuminating, chances are you will safely get to your destination. The same goes for reaching goals in sports.

To help your team attain "now" goals, come up with precise objectives for every practice session and competition. For example, a volleyball team could focus on communicating loud and clear on offence during a game, picking specific targets before serving and using mindful breathing to calm down between rallies.

To help the team direct their efforts and focus, make the daily goals known before starting a session, either by saying them out loud, writing them on a board or sending them by a text messaging app. Younger athletes are very connected to their technology and this may be the best way to communicate with them. Achieving daily goals, over and over again, will increase the team's chances of reaching the year-end goal.

INCLUDE THE ATHLETES

When I worked at Cirque du Soleil, we always included the artists when discussing and setting goals. It was part of the culture. I liked the idea of having the artists involved in the discussion so much that I adopted the same approach when working with Olympians. The figure skating duo Scott Moir and Tessa Virtue were included not only when we discussed objectives for the year, but they also ran the meetings most of the time. Their opinions were vital when constructing optimal training programs and considering ideas such as including extra rest during large training blocks to encourage recovery — as well as to avoid injury or having old injuries reappear — was a team decision. With their input, we were able to reach the goals and conquer Olympic gold.

When dealing with younger athletes, you will have to adjust your goal-setting discussions to fit the age and stage of development for this group. This will allow you to better direct these conversations and steer the athletes towards realistic goals. Including them in goal-getting sessions will be a valuable growth experience for them and over time they will provide more relevant feedback. Coaches may have to experiment with the degree of involvement of their younger athletes, but you have to start the process and adjust according to the needs of the group.

CREATE INTERNAL COMPETITION

Have you heard the story about two best friends who come face to face with a bear in the forest? One turns and begins running. The other yells, "You really think you can outrun the bear?" His friend responds, "I don't need to outrun the bear, I just need to outrun you!"

Occasionally, teammates are also best friends. However, when competition starts and there is something at stake, a competitive athlete will want to become better than their teammate. When you were competing, did you ever hope a teammate underperformed or got injured so you could have more playing time? Many athletes have that thought at some point. To get a team to reach the top, you must find a way to create a healthy internal competition. Here are a few suggestions:

- Have athletes do individual drills beside someone else. For example, in a 60-metre dash, an athlete will tend to push themselves harder when running it with a teammate, compared to running it alone. Instinctively, it brings the competitor out of the athlete.
- When drills involve two individuals, match athletes strategically to push them in training. For American football, match your best receiver to your best defender to make it hard for both to succeed. This increases the level of challenge and will make the players better. The same can be said for volleyball; match the best attacker with the best blocker. In soccer, put the best striker against the best goalkeeper. And in baseball, put the best pitcher against the best hitter. Make the drills hard!

REMEMBER INDIVIDUAL GOALS

In a team sport, individualizing goals for each athlete on the team is often forgotten, yet those are just as important as team goals. Why? Because an individual performance will directly impact the team's performance. Plus, every athlete is responsible for their own actions, so having precise goals to focus on will improve their performance. Here are some things to keep in mind when setting individual goals within a team:

- If you have 20 athletes in your program, this means your attention is constantly divided into 20 segments.

It is difficult to remember each athlete's personal goals. To help you be mindful of what athletes are striving to achieve, encourage them to share their personal goals with you and ask them to repeat them to you regularly. Be sure these goals are documented so athletes and coaches can regularly refer to them.

- Have the athletes share their individual goals with their teammates. Biologically, humans are made to help other humans. If an athlete is aware of their teammate's personal goal — such as scoring 30 goals in the season — chances are they will act purposefully to help them achieve it.

- Encourage athletes to come up with three specific goals per practice or competition. From experience, I have noticed that two goals are not enough and four is a little too much. Paying attention to three goals is a perfect number and allows athletes to execute them effectively. Recently, a hockey player I work with came up with these goals:

    - build up speed through the neutral zone,
    - be aware of surroundings in defensive zone and
    - shoot while in stride to disguise my shot.

- After every period, quarter or half (and at breaks during practices), athletes should reflect on their goals to determine if they are executing them according to their plan.

André discovered a creative way to embrace individual goals. On a team, each player usually has a specific role. While some have starting roles and get lots of playing time, others have backup duties and play less. Backup players, or role players, sometimes lack motivation to get better because they feel undervalued on the team.

André found a solution: he used a comparison system. For example, he challenged the team's backup catcher to become the best backup catcher in the world: "Work harder and smarter than all the other backup catchers from other nations." He did the same with a pinch runner, a player who comes into a game to run the bases for another that is likely a slower runner. It gave more meaning to their respective roles. This strategy also ensured role players came into games ready to play at their best, making the national baseball team even more complete.

Team leaders love coming up with shiny and robust plans at the beginning of a season. So much time, effort and energy are invested in coming up with *the* path to success. But your plan should be a living document and not left in the drawer, collecting dust. Many leaders are not great at putting the plan into action.

So, this year, do yourself a favour: Do not worry so much about goal *setting*. Instead, become obsessed with goal *getting*.

CHAPTER 30: MVP

The scenario is often the same. The season ends and now it is time to hand out the hardware. Parents and friends are invited to a big gala to recognize those who stood out on the team during the past several months. Among the awards are trophies or plaques given to the most valuable player, the top scorer and the one with the most points collected during the season.

It seems like we have held award ceremonies in this same fashion forever. Maybe it is time we revolutionize the manner in which we recognize our athletes.

Keep in mind that young athletes practise their sport for many reasons, such as to have fun, learn a new skill, make friends, be part of a team or to simply get some exercise. The more athletes grow older, the more they and their sport will become competitive. As a coach, it is important to define the meaning of victory and choose appropriate ways to recognize players based on their age group and accomplishment.

Let's consider Sophie, a 14-year-old basketball player. She works hard to improve her game but has never cracked her team's starting lineup. After each tournament, Sophie, demonstrating positive sportsmanship, stays to watch her teammates get recognized for their top performances. She then heads over to her parents in the crowd empty-handed, while teammates and rival players hold their trophies. Yet another reminder of how she is not as good as the others.

Sophie is part of a sports environment that measures success based strictly on results. As Sophie gains no individual awards or recognition for her abilities, her self-esteem can take a hit and she can easily abandon her sport earlier than her peers.

We are not suggesting the system should never acknowledge victory or success. Winning will always be used as a measuring stick in sport; it is inevitable since it is the core of competition. But there is a way we can be creative and provide recognition to athletes who might not be the best on their team. For a coach, it is not even necessary to wait until the end of the season to implement this method.

For example, if effort, communication and leadership are the cornerstones of your team's culture, a coach should recognize these values regularly so your players will live them every day. As the saying goes, "If you're going to talk the talk, you'd better walk the walk." Too often, we see coaches connect these values only to the result of a team performance.

Let's examine how you can reassess and update your player recognition model using some examples you can implement immediately. Looking at a sporting competition statistically, the media often presents the same figures when evaluating a performance: the number of goals, assists and points. A coach must also acknowledge additional indicators that will stress the importance of other players on the team and align with the team culture. Such qualities or abilities may get passed over by the casual observer, but skilled coaches have a keen eye for these and know how to highlight their importance.

During my years as a baseball coach, I always carried my old green T-shirt with the words "Awesomeness on the field" marked

Reward
what
matters
most.

on it. After each game of a World Cup tournament, I would award the shirt to our team's top defensive player. This recognition could be given to a player who might have made only one play but still had a significant impact on the outcome of the game. For example, a player may have made a nice play to end an inning and prevent our opponent from scoring a run, or several runs. In baseball, the media do not always emphasize defence. Even though stellar defence can grab everyone's attention, it is the offensive performances or those of the starting pitcher that often make the headlines. That is why, for me, defensive contribution became a very important achievement to recognize. Over time, the formula evolved. One day, after the green T-shirt had been handed out, another player decided to conduct a mock interview with the recipient. She grabbed a bat for her microphone and the show began:

"I'm here with Martine, winner of the green T-shirt. Martine, how would you describe your effort today?" Martine played along with the interview, answering each question as the entire team smiled and laughed while watching.

Teams in professional sports have gotten creative with using different items to award their top performers in a game, including a firefighter helmet for the Calgary Flames and a superhero cape for the Montreal Canadiens in the NHL. The post-game ritual might symbolize player recognition, but it also strengthens a team's bond in the process.

Following my departure from the national team, the new coach replaced my old green T-shirt with an equally effective idea. During his first tournament as head of the program, the team was in Mexico. When they arrived, he purchased a sombrero. The well-known Mexican hat would serve as the new green T-shirt, only with a twist: The deserving player would have to make an improvement to the sombrero before returning it to the coach the next day before the game. The addition could be a feather, a pin, fake glasses or any other funny decoration. You can imagine how the weight of the hat increased as the weeklong tournament rolled along, but so did the team's chemistry.

What are some other performance indicators you can consider for your team in order to create a more expanded awards model? Is it possible to measure these standards objectively? Perhaps you can address other elements such as:

- time of possession
- total penalty minutes
- number of technical fouls
- total scoring chances

Allow me to propose a challenge.

Throughout my experience coaching baseball, I was able to identify certain elements that would help determine victory. If accomplished in a game, the 10 items in the chart below would dramatically enhance a team's chances of winning:

Keys to Victory Chart	
Elements	**Execution?**
Scoring five runs	
Having a total of at least twelve baserunners	
Getting at least eight base hits	
Getting two or more extra base hits	
Scoring at least two runs with two outs	
Pitchers throwing a strike on first pitch 70% of the time	
Hitters striking out four times or less	
Lead-off hitter getting on base at least four times	
Getting at least two base hits with two strikes	
Executing at least one plus play defensively (e.g. double play)	

Can you determine the components required for your team that would create a recipe for success? Browsing your list, can you also ensure the majority of your team's players would be able to contribute to completing the to-do list?

This program could also become part of a team custom where, once all goals on the list have been achieved, the player who completes the final objective gets to tape the list to the team bench or post it on the wall for everyone to see. The victory chart will generate pride and serve as a shared responsibility for the entire group. It challenges all team members to make a contribution that will have bearing on the overall result.

As mentioned at the start of this chapter, coaches and organizations often fall into the trap of tradition when planning award ceremonies. Here are some examples of categories that can inspire and encourage other accomplishments during a season, beyond simply determining a team's MVP.

MUP (MOST UNIFYING PLAYER)

Given to the player who best displays team spirit and energy around teammates. Without their presence, there would be no glue holding the group together, nor any passion or intensity in the air. This individual communicates with the entire group through uplifting words and actions that place the common good ahead of their own needs.

MPP (MOST PERSEVERANT PLAYER)

Awarded to the individual on the team who never quits. This athlete is always ready for a challenge and contributes to the success of the group through their fiery spirit and resiliency. Such a player is the type you'd love to have on your team but would hate to face. This athlete is often in the game when the tide turns and a team needs a spark to reverse its fortunes.

MCP (MOST CURIOUS PLAYER)

This individual asks the most questions during a season. Their curiosity displayed throughout the season helps foster creativity during practice and game preparation sessions, making the team more competitive and the players more well-rounded.

MRP (MOST RESPECTFUL PLAYER)

Given to the athlete who is always available to others, listening to their concerns and offering solutions. This person seems to always be involved in resolving conflicts among teammates and sometimes fixing problems without others even knowing that an issue exists.

MOP (MOST OOPS PLAYER)

This player shows the greatest improvement along the course of the season, taking risks while bouncing back from mistakes with a renewed commitment. The recipient refuses to give up and is always open to feedback. They perform to win, not to avoid failure.

MSP (MOST SOCIAL PLAYER)

Awarded to the player who is always ready to organize a social activity for the team. Whether it is a team supper at a restaurant, a fundraiser in the community, uniform selection or any other idea, this individual will never turn down a chance to build a social bond for the group.

Be creative when introducing your own team M?P. Do not worry about veering off-course and taking the road less travelled. Go ahead and track the characteristics that do not often get recognized. We now live in a time where statistics and analytics have taken over sports. You can use this to your advantage.

Developing a model featuring different forms of recognition will carry impact and encourage your entire team, while indirectly allowing you to obtain a more satisfying degree of success as a unit. We guarantee it.

CONCLUSION

It is incredible to think that, from start to finish, it took over four years for this book to come to life. Patience was our virtue to finally get it done. In full transparency, writing this book was a challenging feat, and to find inspiration, we kept reminding ourselves about the opportunity we had to influence the coaching community around the world — that was enough to get us excited, to push through and to keep writing.

From the start, our objective was never to prescribe a formula to build a sports team because, realistically, there is no clear path to success. However, the elements we share in our periodic table offer some fundamental guidelines to help teams work better as a unit. The idea here is for you, the coach, to take some of these elements and make them your own, based on your coaching philosophy and your personal values. So please, feel free to take the content shared in this book, tweak it, modify it or take it as it is; or even better, come up with your own periodic table to maximize chemistry within your team.

Coaching a sports team is a real privilege. Your leadership duties and responsibilities put you in a situation where, every day, you have an opportunity to impact young individuals' lives significantly. Whether you choose to or not, you become a role model for athletes. Never ever forget that. You must create a positive environment that will create memorable moments for everyone on the team, and we hope that our book can help you achieve that goal.

Fundamentally, you, the leader, should be held accountable if the team gels . . . or not. You must take ownership of this important responsibility. As you know, real chemistry rarely forms on its own — it must be strategically planned.

Our message to you is plain and simple: if you want to achieve something new, you need to consider new ways of doing things. From reading this book, you may have enjoyed some of our concepts, approaches and techniques, but if you never consider using them, you will never know how they may help your team reach its full potential.

So, all that being said, what will you do now with the knowledge you just learned?

- Are you willing to reconsider your coaching habits, philosophies and beliefs?
- Are you comfortable implementing new ways of doing things?
- Are you ready to make mistakes or to feel vulnerable for the betterment of the team?

In the immortal words of Yoda, the legendary Jedi Master: "Do or do not, there is no try."

ACKNOWLEDGEMENTS

Success in sport only happens with the presence of remarkable athletes, so we would like to start by thanking all the athletes and performers we worked with over the years. You gave us the opportunity to practice professions we love. Your openness and trust in our expertise (and sometimes wild ideas!) don't go unnoticed.

Thank you to all staff members — assistant coaches, therapists, equipment managers, media attachés, administrators and everyone else who played vital roles in all teams we were part of. These people deserve a lot more credit than they receive. Please know that you have impacted the content in this book in one way or another.

This book would never have seen the light of day without the partnership with ECW Press. Your expertise and guidance turned our ideas into a fantastic book. To the whole team at ECW Press, thank you.

Last but not least, thank you to our families for your undeniable support throughout the entire process. We were able to write this book with very few distractions because of your patience. Thank you for letting us live our passion. We are truly blessed.

André Lachance is an internationally acclaimed baseball coach who built Canada's first Women's National Program and has led the team to second place in the world rankings. In 2019, he was named head coach of France's National Women's Team, capturing the European Championship. He was the business and sport development director at Baseball Canada and is an award-winning professor in the School of Human Kinetics at the University of Ottawa. André is based in Gatineau, Québec, Canada.

Jean François Ménard is an internationally acclaimed mental performance expert who coaches high achievers in all walks of life. His clients are proven winners: Olympic gold medalists, Super Bowl and X Games champions, Cirque du Soleil artists, pop stars and corporate leaders. He is the founder of Kambio Performance, a company specializing in mental training and leadership coaching. He is also the bestselling author of *Train (Your Brain) Like an Olympian*, a media personality and an accomplished speaker who shares his knowledge with elite organizations like the FBI, NASA, Red Bull, PepsiCo and RBC. He is based in Montréal, Québec, Canada.

"Ménard is a leader in the field. His book teaches the importance of mental training and how it can help you step up your game when the heat is on."
— **PAT BRISSON**, NHLPA agent,
Co-Head of CAA Hockey

"Thanks to the mental training techniques shared in the book, we overcame our fears and gave it our best shot on the ice. There's no greater gift for an athlete!"
— **SCOTT MOIR** and **TESSA VIRTUE**,
figure skaters, three-time Olympic champions

This book is also available as a Global Certified Accessible™ (GCA) ebook. ECW Press's ebooks are screen reader friendly and are built to meet the needs of those who are unable to read standard print due to blindness, low vision, dyslexia, or a physical disability.

At ECW Press, we want you to enjoy our books in whatever format you like. If you've bought a print copy just send an email to ebook@ecwpress.com and include:

- the book title
- the name of the store where you purchased it
- a screenshot or picture of your order/receipt number and your name
- your preference of file type: PDF (for desktop reading), ePub (for a phone/tablet, Kobo, or Nook), mobi (for Kindle)

A real person will respond to your email with your ebook attached. Please note this offer is only for copies bought for personal use and does not apply to school or library copies.

Thank you for supporting an independently owned Canadian publisher with your purchase!